GERMAN GRAMMAR
Your Guide
Fifth edition

Val Levick
Glenise Radford
Alasdair McKeane

CONTENTS

Grammatical Terms Explained 1

Adjectives
    Adjectives not followed by a Noun 6
    Adjectives followed by a Noun 6
    Adjectives which do not take an ending 8
    Adjectives used as Nouns 8
    Adjectives which take the Dative 8
    Adjectives with Prepositions 9
    Nothing and Something 9

Adverbs
    Adverbs of Place 10
    Adverbs of Direction 10
    Adverbs of Manner 11
    Adverbs of Degree 11
    Question Words 11
    Adverbs of Time 11

Articles
    Definite 12
    Indefinite 13

Cases
    Nominative 15
    Accusative 15
    Genitive 16
    Dative 17

Comparisons   18

Conjunctions
    Co-ordinating Conjunctions 20
    Subordinating Conjunctions 20

Dates and Times
    Days 22
    Months 22
    Dates 22
    Clock Times 23
    Definite and Indefinite Time 24

Contents

Nouns	Gender	25
	Masculine by Form	25
	Feminine by Form	25
	Neuter by Form	25
	Masculine by Meaning	26
	Feminine by Meaning	26
	Neuter by Meaning	27
	Unhelpful Genders of Names of Human Beings	28
	Compound Words	28
	Loan Words from English	28
	Nouns with More than one Gender	28
	Plural Forms	28
	Masculine Nouns	28
	Feminine Nouns	29
	Neuter Nouns	29
	Loan Words from English	29
	Declension of Nouns	29
	Spelling Changes	29
	Weak Nouns	29
Numbers	Cardinal Numbers	31
	Cardinal Numbers: the finer points	32
	Ordinal Numbers - Formation	32
	Ordinal Numbers - Usage	33
	Fractions	33
Prepositions	Which take the Accusative	34
	Which take the Dative	34
	Which take either the Dative or Accusative	35
	Which take the Genitive	36
Pronouns	Personal Pronouns	37
	Reflexive Pronouns	38
	Du or Sie?	38
	Er, sie and es	39
	Relative Pronouns	39
	Interrogative Pronouns	41
	Demonstrative Pronouns	42
Spelling and Punctuation	Spelling	43
	Punctuation	43
Word Order	Verbs	45
	Time, Manner, Place	46
	Dative and Accusative	47

Contents

Verbs

- Persons 48
- Forms of German Verbs 48
- Weak, Strong and Mixed Verbs 48
- Present Tense 49
- Future Tense 51
- Perfect Tense 52
- Imperfect Tense 54
- Formation of the Imperfect 55
- Pluperfect Tense 56
- The Passive Voice 57
- Conditions 62
- The Subjunctive 63
- Command Forms (Imperatives) 64
- Modal Verbs 65
- The Infinitive 70
- Participles 73
- Verbs Followed by the Nominative 74
- Verbs Followed by the Dative 75
- Impersonal Verbs 75
- Reflexive Verbs 76
- Separable Verbs 77
- Inseparable Verbs 79
- Verbs Followed by a Preposition 80
- Regular (Weak) Verbs 82
- Verb Table 84

Index
.... 90

Abbreviations

- * These verbs take **sein** in the perfect and other compound tenses
- *sep* These verbs have a *sep*arable prefix
- *insep* These verbs have an *insep*arable prefix
- **masc** masculine
- **fem** feminine
- (pl) plural
- *(no pl)* no plural
- **Nom** nominative
- **Acc** accusative
- **Gen** genitive
- **Dat** dative

GRAMMATICAL TERMS EXPLAINED

Grammatical terms are frequently thought of as boring and/or confusing, but, in reality, they need be neither. Once you have sorted out in your mind what they mean and what they do, you will realise that they are helpful, user-friendly tools which can help you with your language learning.
In this list you will find, arranged in alphabetical order, some of the terms you are likely to meet.

ADJECTIVES (DIE ADJEKTIVE)

These are words which describe or tell you more about a noun.
There are many kinds of adjectives: *big, green, intelligent, German*
They all serve to give extra information about their noun.

ADVERBS (DIE ADVERBIEN)

These are words which are added to a verb, adjective or another adverb to tell you how, when, where (*quickly, soon, there*) a thing was done.

Two "technical terms" you will encounter with both adjectives and adverbs are **Comparative** and **Superlative**.
Comparative (der Komparativ) is the form of the adjective or adverb used to say that someone or something is *bigger/quicker/more intelligent, etc* than someone or something else.
Superlative (der Superlativ) is the form of the adjective or adverb used to say that someone or something is *best, worst, biggest, most intelligent, etc.*

AGREEMENT (DIE KONGRUENZ)

This is the word used for the way in which adjectives change their endings to agree with or "match" the article (or lack of it) in front of them, and the gender, case and number of the noun they are describing.

ARTICLES (DIE ARTIKEL)

There are two kinds of articles:
    Definite (der bestimmte Artikel):   *the*
    Indefinite (der unbestimmte Artikel): *a, an, some*

CASES (DIE FÄLLE)

All nouns in German can occur in one of four cases,
Nominative (Nominativ), Accusative (Akkusativ), Genitive (Genitiv) or **Dative (Dativ)**.
The case which is used depends on the function of the noun in the sentence.
The same is true of pronouns.

Grammatical Terms   *German Grammar*

CLAUSES (DIE SATZTEILE)

These are parts of a sentence which contain a subject and a verb which agrees with that subject. There are two important sorts of clause in German.
A **main clause (der Hauptsatz)**
could stand alone as a complete sentence making complete sense.
A **subordinate clause (der Nebensatz)**
could not stand alone and make complete sense without being changed.

Example: **main clause**   **subordinate clause**
               I could not phone you   because I was ill

CONJUNCTIONS (DIE KONJUNKTIONEN)

These are words used to join sentences and clauses.
Co-ordinating conjunctions (nebenordnende Konjunktionen)
such as *and, but* and *or* join two main clauses together.
Subordinating conjunctions (Teilsatzkonjunktionen)
such as *because, when, that* and *whether* join a subordinate clause onto a main clause.

GENDER (DAS GENUS)

There are three genders in German:
masculine (Maskulinum), **feminine (Femininum)** and **neuter (Neutrum)**.
All nouns fit into one or other of these categories.

NOUNS (DIE SUBSTANTIVE)

These are names of people, places and things.
They can be either   **proper nouns (die Eigennamen):** *Berlin, Monika*
             or   **common nouns (die Nomen):** *boy, girl, bike, house*

and either **abstract (abstrakte Nomen):** *kindness, anger, justice*
        or   **concrete (konkrete Nomen):** *table, dog, car*

NUMBER (DER NUMERUS)

Things can be   **singular (Einzahl):**   *one only*
           or   **plural (Mehrzahl):**   *two or more*

PREPOSITIONS (DIE PRÄPOSITIONEN)

These are words placed in front of nouns and pronouns to show position and other relationships:
in *the garden,* **between** *the houses,* **on** *the floor*
before *midnight,* **after** *8 o'clock,* **during** *the day*

German Grammar — Grammatical Terms

PRONOUNS (DIE PRONOMEN)
Pronouns fall into one of the following categories:

Demonstrative Pronouns (Demonstrativpronomen):
These pronouns are used to differentiate between   *this/that, these/those*

Direct Object Pronouns (Akkusativpronomen):
These show who or what is the recipient of the verb action:
me, you, him, her, it, us, them.

Indirect Object Pronouns (Dativpronomen):
These are: *to me   to you   to him/her/it   to us   to them*
Example: *I give it **to you***

Indefinite Pronouns (unbestimmte Pronomen):
Example: *each one, someone, everything*

Interrogative Pronouns (Fragewörter):
These ask questions:
Example: *Who?*

Personal Pronouns (Personalpronomen):
This is the general name given to subject, direct object, indirect object and reflexive pronouns.
They can be: first person   *I, me, we, us*
second person   *you*
third person   *he, him, she, her, they, them*

Relative Pronouns (Relativpronomen):
These pronouns introduce a clause giving more information about a noun:
who, which, that

Subject Pronouns (Nominativpronomen):
These pronouns show who is performing the action of the verb:
I, you, he, she, it, one, we, you, they

VERBS (DIE VERBEN)

German verbs are relatively straightforward.
A verb will tell you the actions and events in a sentence.
Example: *Ich **spiele** Fußball*   *I **am playing** football*
  *Val **ist** am Bahnhof **angekommen***   *Val **arrived** at the station*
  *Wir **hörten** Radio*   *We **were listening** to the radio*

There are some "technical" words which are used when talking about verbs:

Infinitive (der Infinitiv)
This is the "name" of the verb. It is the form which is listed in a dictionary or verb table. It means:-   "to ..."
Example: **hören** - *to listen to,* ***to hear***

Conjugation (die Konjugation)

This is the term used to describe the different forms, tenses, moods and persons of the verb. It is also the name given to the pattern which verbs follow. German verbs are either **regular (weak)**, **irregular (strong)** or **"mixed"** (behaving like weak verbs but with vowel changes like strong verbs).

Irregular Verbs/Strong Verbs (unregelmäßige Verben)

These verbs can have a vowel change in the present, imperfect and perfect tense and in German the past participle often ends in **-en**. They are set out for you in the verb table at the back of this book. (see page 84) They are verbs which are frequently used and which you **must** know.

    Example: **essen** *to eat*   **fahren** *to drive*   **singen** *to sing*

Regular Verbs/Weak Verbs (regelmäßige Verben)

These verbs follow a set pattern.
There is no vowel change and in German their past participle ends in -t.
Many of the common ones are listed on pages 82/83.

    Example: **spielen** *to play*   **arbeiten** *to work*   **besuchen** *to visit*

Subject (das Subjekt)

This is the person or thing performing the action of the verb.
The subject can be either a noun or a pronoun:
    Example: ***The children*** *find the dog.* ***They*** *chase it*

Object (das Okjekt)

This is the person or thing affected by the action of the verb.
The object of the sentence can be either a noun or a pronoun:
    Example: *They eat* ***the apples*** *We saw* ***them***

Tenses (die Zeiten)

Tenses are the methods by which verbs tell you **when** events take place, will take place, took place, used to take place, etc.
The names of the tenses are a guide to their use:

The **Present (das Präsens)** tense tells you what *is happening now,* or what *usually happens*

The **Future (das Futur)** tells you what *will happen*

The **Perfect (das Perfekt)** and **Imperfect (das Präteritum)** tell you what *has happened* or *was happening* in the past

The **Pluperfect (das Plusquamperfekt)** tells you what *had happened* or what *had been happening*

Past Participle (das Partizip Perfekt)

This is part of a verb used with an **auxiliary verb (Hilfsverb)**, *haben* or *sein*, to form the **Perfect** and **Pluperfect** tenses.
In English it often ends in **-en, -ed or -t**
   given, looked, bought
In German, for weak (regular) and "mixed" verbs it ends in **-t**:
   gemacht, repariert
For strong (irregular) verbs the past participle is irregular. Many past participles also have a vowel change. They have to be learned carefully.
   gegessen, gefahren

Present Participle (das Partizip Präsens)

These are a part of the verb which ends in **-ing** in English, and **-end** in German. It is best to use them only as adjectives or nouns.

   Example: *der sing**end**e Auszubildende*

Reflexive Verbs (reflexive Verben)

These are verbs which have an extra pronoun:

   Example: *Ich wasche **mich***

Imperatives or Commands (der Imperativ)

These are the forms of the verb you use when you are telling somebody to do something:
   Geh(e) *nach Hause!*   Go home!
   Geht *nach Hause!*   Go home!
   Gehen Sie *nach Hause!* Go home!
   Gehen wir *nach Hause!* Let's go home!
The one you choose is dictated by who you are speaking to.

Active or Passive (Aktiv oder Passiv)

Verbs can be either active or passive.
Active means that the subject performs the action:

   Example: *Sie hat den Hund im Park gefunden*
             She found the dog in the park

Passive means that the subject has the verb action done to it:

   Example: *Der Hund wurde im Park gefunden*
             The dog was found in the park

The Passive is used much more often in German than in English.

ADJECTIVES (DIE ADJEKTIVE)

ADJECTIVES NOT FOLLOWED BY A NOUN (ALLEINSTEHENDE ADJEKTIVE)

Adjectives which stand alone - usually after **sein**, **werden** and **scheinen** - do not have an adjective ending.

    Example: Der Mann ist klein   *The man is small*

Tip: Students who are also learning French sometimes follow the French habit of making adjectives standing alone agree. This is WRONG in German.

ADJECTIVES FOLLOWED BY A NOUN (ADJEKTIVE UND SUBSTANTIVE)

Adjectives followed by a noun agree with ("match") the noun by taking an ending which depends on four factors:

    (a) the article (determiner) or lack of one in front of the adjective
    (b) the gender of the noun - masculine, feminine, or neuter
    (c) the case of the noun - nominative, accusative, genitive or dative
    (d) whether the noun is singular or plural

If there is more than one adjective before the noun, each one agrees. Once one ending has been worked out in these circumstances, all the others in front of the same noun will have the same ending.

There are three tables (sets) of adjective endings.
The one to use depends on which article (determiner) is used:

Table 1:

After **der/die/das,** etc *the,* **dieser** *this,* **jener** *that,* **jeder** *each/every,* **welcher** *which,* **solcher** *such a,* **mancher** *many a* and **alle** *all (which is plural)*

	Masculine Singular	Feminine Singular	Neuter Singular
Nominative:	der kleine Mann	die kleine Frau	das kleine Kind
Accusative:	den kleinen Mann	die kleine Frau	das kleine Kind
Genitive:	des kleinen Mannes	der kleinen Frau	des kleinen Kindes
Dative:	dem kleinen Mann(e)	der kleinen Frau	dem kleinen Kind(e)

	Plural, all genders
Nominative:	die kleinen Leute
Accusative:	die kleinen Leute
Genitive:	der kleinen Leute
Dative:	den kleinen Leuten

Tips:
- All Genitive and Dative Singular and all Plural endings are **-en**.
- Masculine and Neuter nouns in the Genitive singular have **-es** or **-s** added.
- Single-syllable Masculine and Neuter nouns in the Dative Singular can have **-e** added in formal writing.
- Remember to add **-n** to nouns which do not already have one in the Dative Plural of all genders.

German Grammar — Adjectives

Table 2:

After **ein/eine/ein** *a*, **kein** *no*, and the Possessive Adjectives, **mein** *my*, **dein** *your* (familiar singular), **sein** *his/its*, **ihr** *her/its*, **unser** *our*, **euer** *your* (familiar plural), **Ihr** *your* (polite singular or plural) and **ihr** *their*, the adjective has the following endings:

	Masculine Singular	Feminine Singular	Neuter Singular
Nominative:	ein klein**er** Mann	eine klein**e** Frau	ein klein**es** Kind
Accusative:	einen klein**en** Mann	eine klein**e** Frau	ein klein**es** Kind
Genitive:	eines klein**en** Mann**es**	einer klein**en** Frau	eines klein**en** Kind**es**
Dative:	einem klein**en** Mann**(e)**	einer klein**en** Frau	einem klein**en** Kind**(e)**

Plural, all genders

Nominative:	keine klein**en** Leute
Accusative:	keine klein**en** Leute
Genitive:	keiner klein**en** Leute
Dative:	keinen klein**en** Leute**n**

Tips:
- For reasons of logic, **ein** itself has no plural. If "a" is plural (ie "some"), it follows the plural pattern for Table 3 given below.
- All Genitive and Dative Singular and all Plural endings are **-en**.
- Masculine and Neuter nouns in the Genitive singular have **-es** or **-s** added.
- Single-syllable Masculine and Neuter nouns in the Dative Singular can have **-e** added in formal writing.
- Remember to add **-n** to nouns which do not already have one in the Dative Plural of all genders.

Table 3:

Adjectives which are used alone before the noun have the following endings:

	Masculine Singular	Feminine Singular	Neuter Singular
Nominative:	gut**er** Wein	gut**e** Milch	gut**es** Bier
Accusative:	gut**en** Wein	gut**e** Milch	gut**es** Bier
Genitive:	gut**en** Weins	gut**er** Milch	gut**en** Biers
Dative:	gut**em** Wein	gut**er** Milch	gut**em** Bier

Plural, all genders†

Nominative:	gut**e** Getränke
Accusative:	gut**e** Getränke
Genitive:	gut**er** Getränke
Dative:	gut**en** Getränke**n**

† also after non-specific numbers: **viele** *many*, **mehrere** *several*, **einige** *a few*, **ein paar** *a few* and numbers

Tip: The ending **-en** in the Genitive singular for masculine and neuter adjectives might seem a little odd, but is RIGHT.

Adjectives *German Grammar*

ADJECTIVES WHICH DO NOT TAKE AN ENDING (UNVERÄNDERLICHE ADJEKTIVE)

(a) Some colours and a few other words borrowed from other languages do not take an ending. These include: beige, lila, orange, rosa *pink*, sexy

(b) Those formed from town names always end in -er and add no further ending:

    Example: am Frankfurter Flughafen   *at Frankfurt airport*

ADJECTIVES USED AS NOUNS (ADJEKTIVE ALS SUBSTANTIVE)

Many adjectives and participles can be used as nouns in German. They are then written with a capital letter.

    Example: der Deutsche/die Deutsche   *the German*

Adjective-type nouns take the same endings as they would if they were followed by a noun of the appropriate gender.

Example:

like Table 1:	**Masculine Singular**	**Feminine Singular**	**Plural**
Nominative:	der Deutsche	die Deutsche	die Deutschen
Accusative:	den Deutschen	die Deutsche	die Deutschen
Genitive:	des Deutschen	der Deutschen	der Deutschen
Dative:	dem Deutschen	der Deutschen	den Deutschen

like Table 2:	**Masculine Singular**	**Feminine Singular**	**Plural** (like Table 3)
Nominative:	ein Deutscher	eine Deutsche	Deutsche
Accusative:	einen Deutschen	eine Deutsche	Deutsche
Genitive:	eines Deutschen	einer Deutschen	Deutscher
Dative:	einem Deutschen	einer Deutschen	Deutschen

ADJECTIVES WHICH TAKE THE DATIVE (ADJEKTIVE MIT DATIV)

A number of adjectives are always used with the Dative case. Usually these adjectives come after the noun to which they refer.

The common ones are listed here:

behilflich	*helpful to*	klar	*obvious*
bekannt	*known to*	möglich	*possible*
dankbar	*grateful to*	peinlich	*embarrassing*
fremd	*strange*	wichtig	*important*

    Example: Es ist **dem Lehrer** klar
                   It is clear to the teacher

Tip: Many of these can be translated by *to me* in English. This is much the same idea as the Dative.

    Example: Es ist **mir** peinlich
                   *It is embarrassing **to me/for me***

Adjectives with Prepositions (Adjektive mit Prepositionen)

A large number of adjectives have a preposition between themselves and a noun. **Auf** and **über** always take the Accusative in this circumstance.

Some common adjective + preposition combinations are:

böse auf + Acc	*cross with*
dankbar für + Acc	*thankful for*
erstaunt über + Acc	*amazed about*
gewöhnt an + Acc	*accustomed to*
interessiert an + Acc	*interested in*
neugierig auf + Acc	*curious about*
stolz auf + Acc	*proud of*
typisch für + Acc	*typical of*
zuständig für + Acc	*responsible for*
böse mit + Dat	*cross with*
einverstanden mit + Dat	*agreeable to*
fertig mit + Dat	*to have finished with*
verschieden von + Dat	*different from*

Nothing and Something (Nichts und Etwas)

After **nichts** *nothing* and **etwas** *something* the adjective is written with a capital letter and has **-es** added.

Example: nichts **Neues**   *nothing new*
etwas **Gutes**   *something good*

An exception is the idiom:

alles Gute!   *Best Wishes*

ADVERBS (ADVERBIEN)

Adverbs (they "add information" to a verb, an adverb or an adjective) present few problems in German. Most adjectives can be used as adverbs without any change.

Example: Er fährt **schnell**
         *He drives **quickly***

There are different types of adverbs: of place, direction, manner, degree and time, as well as question words.

ADVERBS OF PLACE (LOKALADVERBIEN)

(a) **Hier, dort** and **da** translate as *here, there* and *there*

Example: **Hier** im Bild ist mein Sohn, **dort** ist meine Frau und **da** ist unser Haus
__Here__ is my son in the picture, __there__ is my wife and __there__ is our house

(b) **Oben, unten** translate as *upstairs* and *downstairs*

Example: **Oben** ist sie nicht. Sie ist also **nach unten** gegangen
She isn't __upstairs__. She has therefore gone __downstairs__

(c) **Irgend-** can be tacked onto the front of words to convey the meaning *or other*, thus:

   irgendwo   *somewhere*
   irgendwann   *sometime or other*
   irgendwie   *somehow*

Example: **Irgend**etwas stimmt nicht
__Something or other__ is not right
Wir sehen uns wieder, **irgend**wo, **irgend**wann
We'll meet again, __somewhere, sometime__

ADVERBS OF DIRECTION (LOKALADVERBIEN)

Many adverbs and prepositions can have **hin** or **her** added to them. Generally, **hin** is used for motion away from the speaker, and **her** is used for motion towards the speaker. **Hin** and **her** can also be used like a separable prefix to show movement.

Example: Wo**hin** fährst du?
__Where__ are you going __(to)__?
Wo**her** kommst du?
__Where__ do you come __from__?
Geht **hin**ein! *Go in!*
Kommt **her**ein! *Come in!*
Komm mal **her**! *Come here!*

Adverbs of Manner (Adverbien der Art und Weise)

Many adverbs of manner do not occur as adjectives.

These include:

ebenfalls	likewise,	möglicherweise	possibly
ebenfalls	the same to you	normalerweise	normally
glücklicherweise	fortunately	sicherlich	surely
hoffentlich	hopefully	sonst	otherwise
immerhin	all the same	umsonst	in vain
komischerweise	funnily	vielleicht	perhaps
leider	unfortunately	zweifellos	doubtless

Adverbs of Degree (Adverbien des Grades)

These include:

außerordentlich	extraordinarily	mäßig	moderately
besonders	especially	relativ	relatively
etwas	rather	sehr	very
fast	almost	völlig	completely
ganz	quite	wahrscheinlich	probably
genug	enough	ziemlich	fairly
kaum	hardly	zu	too

Tip: Making sure you know more than just *sehr* is a very easy way of making your writing seem more sophisticated.

Adverbs of Time (Adverbien der Zeit)

heute	today	manchmal	sometimes
gestern	yesterday	morgens	in the morning
morgen	tomorrow	abends	in the evening
oft	often	nachts	in the night

Question Words (Fragewörter)

These include:

Wo?	Where?	Wann?	When?
Wohin?	Where to?	Bis wann?	Until when, By when?
Woher?	Where from?	Seit wann?	Since when?
Von wo?	Where from?	Wie lange?	How long?
		Wie oft?	How often?
Wie?	How?		
Warum?	Why?		
Wozu?	What ... for?		
Wovon?	From where? Of what?		
Weshalb?	Why?		
Womit?	With what?		
Woraus?	From where? Out of what?		

ARTICLES (DIE ARTIKEL)

THE DEFINITE ARTICLE (DER BESTIMMTE ARTIKEL)

Pattern of the definite article

	Masculine	Feminine	Neuter	Plural
Nominative:	der	die	das	die
Accusative:	den	die	das	die
Genitive:	des (s)	der	des (s)	der
Dative:	dem	der	dem	den (n)

Note that the noun in the Genitive masculine and neuter singular also adds an **-s** or **-es**.

Example: ein Foto des Wagens *a photo of the car*

Note also that the noun in the Dative plural adds an **n** (unless it already ends in **n** or **s**).

Example: mit den Fahrrädern *with the bikes*

Other words following the 'der/die/das' pattern

	Masculine	Feminine	Neuter	Plural	Meaning
Nominative:	dieser	diese	dieses	diese	*this*
	jener	jene	jenes	jene	*that*
	jeder	jede	jedes	jede	*each, every*
	welcher	welche	welches	welche	*which*
	solcher	solche	solches	solche	*such (a)*
	mancher	manche	manches	manche	*many (a)*
				alle	*all*

Use of the Definite Article

The definite article is required in German in the following circumstances, when it would not be used in English.

(a) before nouns expressing periods of time or meals

Example: **der** Herbst — *Autumn*
im Herbst — *in Autumn*
im August — *in August*
am Montag — *on Monday*
nach **dem** Frühstück — *after breakfast*

(b) before names of countries which are feminine or plural

Example: aus **der** Schweiz — *from Switzerland*
in **der** Bundesrepublik — *in Germany*

(c) before abstract nouns

Example: **Die** Zeit vergeht schnell — *Time passes quickly*

(d) with prices

    Example: 5 Euro **das** Kilo   *5 euros a kilo*
                  10 Cent **das** Stück   *10 cents each*

(e) when a proper noun is preceded by an adjective

    Example: **das** vereinigte Deutschland   *unified Germany*

(f) when infinitives are used as nouns

    Example: **Das** Schwimmen macht Spaß *Swimming is fun*

(g) in certain specific phrases

    Example: mit **der** Bahn   *by train*
                  mit **dem** Bus   *by bus*
                  in **die** Schule   *to school*
                  zur Schule   *to school*
                  in **der** Schule   *in school*
                  ins Bett   *to bed*
                  im Bett   *in bed*
                  in **die** Kirche   *to church*
                  in **der** Kirche   *in church*
                  in **die** Stadt   *into town*
                  in **der** Stadt   *in town*

THE INDEFINITE ARTICLE (DER UNBESTIMMTE ARTIKEL)

Pattern of the Indefinite Article

	Masculine	**Feminine**	**Neuter**	**Plural**
Nominative:	ein	eine	ein	keine
Accusative:	einen	eine	ein	keine
Genitive:	eines (s)	einer	eines (s)	keiner
Dative:	einem	einer	einem	keinen (n)

Note that the noun in the Genitive masculine and neuter singular also adds an **-s** or **-es**.

    Example: ein Foto meines Bruder**s** *a photo of my brother*

Note also that the noun in the Dative plural adds an **-n** (unless it already ends in **-n** or **-s**).

    Example: in keinen Geschäfte**n** *in no shops*

Other words following the 'ein/eine/ein' pattern

	Masculine	Feminine	Neuter	Plural	Meaning
Nominative:	mein	meine	mein	meine	*my*
	dein	deine	dein	deine	*your*
	sein	seine	sein	seine	*his*
	ihr	ihre	ihr	ihre	*her*
	sein	seine	sein	seine	*its*
	unser	unsere	unser	unsere	*our*
	euer	eure	euer	eure	*your*
	Ihr	Ihre	Ihr	Ihre	*your*
	ihr	ihre	ihr	ihre	*their*
	kein	keine	kein	keine	*no, not a*

Leaving out the Indefinite Article

There are occasions when the indefinite article is used in English, but not in German.

(a) before nouns denoting a profession or nationality, when no adjective is present.

    Example: Er ist Lehrer   *He is a teacher*
                        Sie ist Deutsche   *She is a German*

    But: Sie ist eine begabte Mathematikerin
               She is a gifted mathematician

(b) in the following common expressions

    Es ist schade   *It's a pity*
    Er ist schlechter Laune   *He's in a bad mood*
    ohne Hut   *without a hat*
    ein Zimmer mit Bad   *a room with a bath*
    Er hat Kopfschmerzen   *He has a headache*

CASES AND THEIR USE (DIE FÄLLE UND IHR GEBRAUCH)

The four cases in German are one of the principal areas of difficulty for English-speaking learners. In fact, the rules for their use are relatively straightforward. Mastering them is a must for the serious student.

THE NOMINATIVE (DER NOMINATIV)

The Nominative case is used:

(a) for the subject of a verb

    Example: **Der Hund** ist krank
              The dog is ill
              Ich wohne in Malvern
              I live in Malvern

Tip: In German the subject is not always the first idea in a sentence.

(b) after the verbs **sein, werden, bleiben, heißen** and **scheinen**

    Example: Du bist und bleibst **ein Esel**
              You are and remain a fool
              Ich werde **ein guter Lehrer**
              I am going to be a good teacher
              Ich heiße **Herr Schmidt**
              My name is Herr Schmidt
              Er scheint **ein fantastischer Gitarrist** zu sein
              He seems to be a fantastic guitarist

THE ACCUSATIVE (DER AKKUSATIV)

The Accusative is used:

(a) for the direct object (the thing that suffers the action of the verb) of active, transitive verbs

    Example: Ich habe **einen Kuli** gekauft   *I bought a biro*
              Es gibt hier **einen Park**   *There is a park here*

(b) after certain prepositions
Some of them may take the Dative in certain circumstances.
See PREPOSITIONS, pages 34-36

(c) for expressions of definite time

    Example: **jeden Tag**   *every day*
              letztes Jahr   *last year*
              nächsten Monat   *next month*

Es hat **den ganzen Tag** geregnet
It rained all day
Freitag, **den 30. November 2007**
Friday 30 November 2007

(d)   for greetings and wishes

Example: **Guten Morgen!**
Good morning!
Fröhliche Weihnachten und **ein glückliches neues Jahr!**
Merry Christmas and a Happy New Year!
Gute Besserung!
Get well soon!
Herzlichen Glückwunsch!
Congratulations!
Herzlichen Glückwunsch zum Geburtstag!
Happy Birthday!

THE GENITIVE (DER GENITIV)

Tip: **von** + Dative is used increasingly in preference to the Genitive to show possession.

Example: Er hörte den Motor **vom Wagen**
He heard the car's engine

The Genitive is used:

(a)   to denote "of" or possession, or an apostrophe *s*

Example: Ein Foto **meiner Schwester**
*A photo **of** my sister*
Das Haus **meiner Großeltern**
My grandparents' house
Der Wagen **meines Bruders**
My brother's car

(b)   the Saxon Genitive, an alternative form similar to English usage, is found with the names of people, towns or countries. Note that there is NO apostrophe in German.

Example: **Frau Krautschneiders** Audi
Frau Krautschneider's Audi

(c)   to show indefinite time
(ie time which it would be impossible to find on a calendar)

Example: **eines sonnigen Frühlingstages**
one sunny Spring day
eines Abends
one evening
eines Nachts   (Note this special use of *die Nacht*)
one night

(d)   in some set phrases:

Example: Einmal **zweiter Klasse** nach Berlin, einfach, bitte
a single second-class ticket to Berlin, please

(e)   after certain prepositions - see PREPOSITIONS, pages 34-36

The Dative (Der Dativ)

The Dative is used:

(a) for the indirect object of a verb

Example: Er gab **seinem Onkel** den Brief
*He gave the letter **to his uncle***

Tip: It is easy to miss the fact that the Dative is needed because it is not always obvious from the English. The example above could be translated as:
He gave his uncle the letter. **Beware!**

(b) after certain prepositions. Some of them may take the Accusative in certain circumstances. See PREPOSITIONS, pages 34-36.

(c) after certain verbs which always take the Dative
The most frequent are **helfen, folgen*** and **danken**.
See also VERBS, page 75.

Example: Ich habe **meinem Vater** in der Küche geholfen
I helped my father in the kitchen
Der Polizist ist **der Frau** gefolgt
The policeman followed the woman
Ich danke **dir**
I thank you

(d) with certain adjectives. See also ADJECTIVES, pages 6-9

Example: Das ist **mir** klar und das ist **ihm** wichtig
That is clear to me and that is important to him

(e) in some impersonal expressions about sensations

Example: **Mir** ist kalt
I am cold
Ihr wurde plötzlich übel
She suddenly felt sick

(f) to show possession, especially with parts of the body or with clothing

Example: Ich habe **mir** die Haare gewaschen
I washed my hair
Jeden Tag ziehe ich **mir** meine Schuluniform an
I put on my school uniform every day

Tip: Note when it is NOT used:
Ich habe mein Auto gewaschen
I washed my car

(g) to express advantage or disadvantage for someone

Example: Peter kaufte **ihr** eine Zeitung
Peter bought a newspaper for her/Peter bought her a newspaper
Man hat **mir** meine Brieftasche gestohlen
They stole my wallet (from me)
Das war **ihnen** kein Problem
It was no problem for them

COMPARISONS (VERGLEICHE)

Adverbs and adjectives can be used in **comparative** (eg *smaller, nicer, more intelligent*) and **superlative** (eg *smallest, nicest, most intelligent*) forms. The patterns below can be used for all adjectives and adverbs. It is wrong to translate literally the English words *more* and *most* into German. In German, the principle is much the same:

Comparative Adjective:
schön *nice*   schöner† *nicer*
intelligent *intelligent*   intelligenter† *more intelligent*

Superlative Adjective:
schön *nice*   der schönste† Tag *the nicest day*
intelligent *intelligent*   das intelligenteste† Kind *the most intelligent child*

† takes the same endings as any other adjective

Comparative Adverb:
schön *nicely*   schöner *in a nicer way*
intelligent *intelligently* intelligenter *in a more intelligent way*

Superlative Adverb:
schön *nicely*   am schönsten *in the nicest manner*
intelligent *intelligently* am intelligentesten *in the most intelligent way*

Example: Die Schüler hier sind **intelligenter** (adjective)
           The students here are more intelligent
           Claire ist **die intelligenteste Studentin** (adjective)
           Claire is the most intelligent student
           Bernard singt heute **schöner** (adverb)
           Bernard is singing better today
           Eddie singt **am schönsten** (adverb)
           Eddie is singing (the) best

Tip: After **-s, -sch, -ß, -t** and **-d,** add **-est** instead of **-st** in the superlative. This does not apply to **größt-**

Example: Heute ist der **heißeste** Tag des Jahres
           Today is the hottest day of the year
           Er ist der **größte** Fußballspieler des Jahrhunderts
           He is the greatest footballer of the century

COMMON EXCEPTIONS (AUSNAHMEN)

(a)   A number of common adjectives with one syllable form comparatives in the usual way, but add an Umlaut.

      Example:

              jung   *young*   jünger   *younger*   der/die/das jüngste   *the youngest*

These include:

alt *old*	kalt *cold*	scharf *sharp*
arm *poor*	klug *clever*	schwach *weak*
dumm *stupid*	kurz *short*	schwarz *black*
groß *large*	lang *long*	stark *strong*
hart *hard*	oft *frequent*	warm *warm*

(b) Some adjectives and adverbs have very irregular comparative and superlative forms.

Adjectives:

gut *good*	besser *better*	der beste *the best*
hoch *high*	höher *higher*	der höchste *the highest*
nah *near*	näher *nearer*	der nächste *the nearest*

Adverbs:

gut *well*	besser *better*	am besten *best*
gern *willingly*	lieber *more willingly*	am liebsten *most willingly*
viel *much*	mehr *more*	am meisten *most of all*

COMPARATIVE SENTENCE PATTERNS (KOMPARATIVSÄTZE)

Note how positive and negative comparisons are expressed.

Example: Er ist aber stärker **als** du
*But he is stronger **than** you*
Ich bin **nicht so** stark **wie** Herkules
*I am **not as** strong **as** Hercules*
Ich bin **genauso** stark **wie** mein Zwillingsbruder
*I am **just as** strong **as** my twin brother*
Er wird **immer** freundlicher
*He is becoming **more and more** friendly*

Tip: Note that the case after **als/wie** is Nominative.

SUPERLATIVE SENTENCE PATTERNS (SUPERLATIVSÄTZE)

Superlatives are expressed in the following ways:

Ich spiele **am besten** Klavier   (adverb)
I play the piano best
Ich bin die **beste** Klavierspielerin der Klasse   (adjective)
I am the best piano player in the class

CONJUNCTIONS (DIE KONJUNKTIONEN)

Conjunctions are words which join two clauses, such as *and, but, because* and *while*. There are two kinds of conjunction in German, known as co-ordinating conjunctions and subordinating conjunctions.

CO-ORDINATING CONJUNCTIONS (NEBENORDNENDE KONJUNKTIONEN)

These join two clauses which could otherwise stand as two German sentences in their own right without any changes being made to them. Most of them can also link single words or phrases in lists. There are five common ones. It is worth learning them well.

Co-ordinating conjunctions have NO effect on word order. They do NOT count in the "1-2-3" rule (see WORD ORDER, page 45), and they do NOT send the verb to the end of the clause.

The five co-ordinating conjunctions are:

und	*and*
aber	*but*
oder	*or*
sondern	*but*
denn	*for*

Example: Er wohnte in Lübeck **und** er hatte dort viele Freunde
He lived in Lübeck and had many friends there

SUBORDINATING CONJUNCTIONS (UNTERORDNENDE KONJUNKTIONEN)

These are conjunctions which add a subordinate clause (ie one which could not stand on its own as a German sentence without any changes being made to it) on to a main clause.

They affect the word order by sending the verb to the end of the clause. If the verb construction includes an auxiliary or modal it comes after the past participle or infinitive.

A subordinate clause is always separated from the main clause by a comma. Unlike in English, the comma has nothing to do with taking breath, but merely marks the fact that there is a subordinate clause.

Example: **Wenn** es heute **regnet**, bleibe ich zu Hause
Ich bleibe zu Hause, **wenn** es heute **regnet**
I shall stay at home if it rains today

Weil ich kein Geld verdient **habe**, kann ich nicht ins Kino gehen
Ich kann nicht ins Kino gehen, **weil** ich kein Geld verdient **habe**
Because I have not earned any money I can't go to the cinema

Weil ich meine Hausafugaben machen **muss**, kann ich nicht kommen
Ich kann nicht kommen, **weil** ich meine Hausaufgaben machen **muss**
I can't come because I've got to do my homework

The common subordinating conjunctions are listed below.

als	*when (single occasion in past)*
bevor	*before*
bis	*until*
da	*as*
damit	*so that*
nachdem	*after (she had done that)*
obgleich	*although*
obwohl	*although*
seitdem	*since*
sobald	*as soon as*
sodass	*in such a way that*
während	*while, whilst*
was	*what*
was für	*what sort of*
weil	*because*
wenn	*if, when, whenever (repeated occasion)*
wie	*as, how*

Tip: There are three words for *when* in German:

wann introduces a question, direct or indirect:

Wann kommst du? (direct)
When are you coming?
Ich möchte gerne wissen, **wann** sie kommt (indirect)
*I would like to know **when** she is coming*

wenn means *if* or *whenever*:

Ich komme mit dem Bus, **wenn** es regnet
*I come by bus **when(ever)** it rains*
*I come by bus **if** it rains*

als refers to a single occasion in the past:

Ich hörte Musik, **als** das Telefon klingelte
*I was listening to music **when** the phone rang*

DATES AND TIMES (DATEN UND ZEITEN)

DAYS (TAGE)

All of these are masculine.

Montag	*Monday*	Freitag	*Friday*
Dienstag	*Tuesday*	Samstag	*Saturday*
Mittwoch	*Wednesday*	Sonnabend	*Saturday*
Donnerstag	*Thursday*	Sonntag	*Sunday*

Note: **am** Montag   *on Monday*

Tip: Don't be fooled by appearances: *Sonnabend* is **Saturday**.

MONTHS (MONATE)

All the months are masculine.

Januar	*January*	Juli	*July*
Februar	*February*	August	*August*
März	*March*	September	*September*
April	*April*	Oktober	*October*
Mai	*May*	November	*November*
Juni	*June*	Dezember	*December*

Note: **im** Februar   *in February*

Tip: *Juni* and *Juli* are often pronounced *Juno* and *Julei* (especially on the telephone) to reduce possible misunderstanding.

DATES (DATEN)

(a)   Asking the date

In speech, the following patterns are used:

> Der wie vielte ist heute? Heute ist der 30. November 2007
> *What is the date today? It's 30 November 2007*
> Am wie vielten beginnen die Ferien? Am 6. Juli
> *When do the holidays begin? On the 6th of July*

In letters, the date is written on the right hand side of the page at the top, like this:

> Berlin, den 1.5.07

German Grammar Dates and Times

(b) There are two correct ways of giving the year.
 Use either: 2008
  or: im Jahre 2008

Tip: In German avoid using **in** 2008 - it's WRONG!

(c) Special days and seasons are:

Neujahr	*New Year's Day*
zu Ostern	*at Easter*
Pfingsten	*Whitsun*
(usually the week **after** the British Spring Bank Holiday)	
der Tag der deutschen Einheit	*German Unification Day* (3rd October)
der Heilige Abend	*Christmas Eve*
der erste Weihnachtstag	*Christmas Day*
der zweite Weihnachtstag	*Boxing Day*
Silvester	*New Year's Eve*

CLOCK TIMES (UHRZEIT)

In German, as in English, there are two ways of telling the time, the everyday way and the 24-hour clock way.

(a) the everyday way

1.00	Es ist ein Uhr
5.00	Es ist fünf Uhr
5.05	Es ist fünf (Minuten) nach fünf
5.15	Es ist Viertel nach fünf
5.30	Es ist halb sechs (*careful!*)
5.45	Es ist Viertel vor sechs
5.55	Es ist fünf (Minuten) vor sechs
12.00	Es ist Mittag/Mitternacht
12.15	Es ist Viertel nach zwölf

(b) the 24-hour clock way

1.00	Es ist ein Uhr
5.00	Es ist fünf Uhr
17.00	Es ist siebzehn Uhr
17.05	Es ist siebzehn Uhr fünf
17.15	Es ist siebzehn Uhr fünfzehn
17.30	Es ist siebzehn Uhr dreißig
17.45	Es ist siebzehn Uhr fünfundvierzig
17.55	Es ist siebzehn Uhr fünfundfünfzig
12.00	Es ist zwölf Uhr
00.01	Es ist null Uhr eins

Dates and Times   German Grammar

DEFINITE AND INDEFINITE TIME (BESTIMMTE UND UNBESTIMMTE ZEIT)

(a) Definite time (which you could find on a calendar if you had to) is shown by using the Accusative case.

It can be used to show a specific time.

Example:
jeden Tag	*every day*
jede Woche	*every week*
jedes Jahr	*every year*
nächste Woche	*next week*
nächstes Jahr	*next year*
letzten Monat	*last month*
letzte Woche	*last week*
letztes Jahr	*last year*

Tip: Count the number of 't's in **letztes**!
There is no '**x**' in **nächstes**

It can also be used to show how long something lasted.

Example: Ich war **den ganzen Tag** in der Schule
I was in school all day

(b) Indefinite time (which you couldn't find on a calendar even if you wanted to) is shown by using the Genitive case.

Example:
eines Tages	*one day*
eines Abends	*one evening*
eines Nachts	*one night*

(Note this special use of **die Nacht**)

(c) Some adverbs ending in **-s** express times.

Example:
abends	*in the evenings*
werktags	*on working days*
montags	*on Mondays*

Note also: tagsüber   *during the day*

NOUNS (SUBSTANTIVE)

GENDER (GENUS)

All German nouns belong to one of three grammatical genders, masculine, feminine, or neuter. Knowing which is which presents a real problem for English-speaking learners. The only really effective solution is to note the gender and the plural form when you first meet a word. Despite first impressions, there are often sensible reasons why a word is one gender or another. The gender is often decided by the last few letters of the word, or by its meaning.

MASCULINE BY FORM (MASKULINUM)

Nouns with the following endings are masculine. Plural forms are given in brackets.

-ant (en)	der Passant	*passer-by*
-ig (e)	der Honig	*honey*
-or (e)	der Motor	*engine*
-ast (e)	der Kontrast	*contrast*
-ismus (no pl)	der Rassismus	*racism*
-us (en)	der Rhythmus	*rhythm*
-ich (e)	der Teppich	*carpet, rug*
-ling (e)	der Frühling	*Spring*

FEMININE BY FORM (FEMININUM)

Nouns with the following endings are feminine. Plural forms are given in brackets.

-a	die Villa (die Villen)	*villa*
-anz (no pl)	die Eleganz	*elegance*
-ei (en)	die Bäckerei	*bakery*
-enz (en)	die Tendenz	*tendency*
-heit (en)	die Kindheit	*childhood*
-ie (n)	die Technologie	*technology*
-ik (no pl)	die Physik	*Physics*
-in (nen)	die Schülerin	*schoolgirl*
-keit (en)	die Freundlichkeit	*friendliness*
-schaft (en)	die Freundschaft	*friendship*
-sion (en)	die Explosion	*explosion*
-sis	die Basis (die Basen)	*basis*
-tion (en)	die Situation	*situation*
-tät (en)	die Universität	*university*
-ung (en)	die Wohnung	*flat*

Exceptions: der Atlantik *Atlantic*   der Katholik *Catholic*   das Sofa *sofa*
der Pazifik *Pacific*   der Papagei *parrot*   das Genie *genius*

NEUTER BY FORM (NEUTRUM)

Nouns with the following endings are neuter. Plural forms are given in brackets.

-chen (-)	das Mädchen	*girl*
-il (e)	das Krokodil	*crocodile*

Nouns   German Grammar

-lein	das Fräulein	*young woman, "miss"*
-ment (s)	das Apartement	*apartment*
-tel	das Viertel	*quarter*
-tum (no pl)	das Eigentum	*property*

MASCULINE BY MEANING

(a) male persons and animals
- der Schüler — *schoolboy*
- der Kater — *tomcat*

(See also UNHELPFUL GENDERS, page 28)

(b) seasons, months and days of the week
- der Sommer — *Summer*
- der August — *August*
- der Sonnabend — *Saturday*

(c) points of the compass, winds, most sorts of weather
- der Süden — *South*
- der Wind — *wind*
- der Regen — *rain*

Exceptions: das Eis *ice*, das Gewitter *thunderstorm*, das Wetter *weather*

(d) alcoholic drinks except das Bier
- der Wein — *wine*
- der Schnaps — *spirits*

(e) makes of car
- der BMW — *(car)*
- der Ford
- der VW

FEMININE BY MEANING

(a) female persons and animals
- die Frau — *woman*
- die Katze — *(female) cat*

(See also UNHELPFUL GENDERS, page 28)

(b) motorcycles, aeroplanes and ships
- die BMW — *(motorcycle)*
- die Boeing
- die "Deutschland"

Exception: der Airbus

(c) names of numerals
- die Sechs — *six*
- die Million — *million*
- die Milliarde — *billion*

German Grammar   *Nouns*

NEUTER BY MEANING

(a) young persons and animals

das Baby	*baby*
das Kind	*child*
das Lamm	*lamb*

(See also UNHELPFUL GENDERS, page 28)

(b) metals and chemical elements

das Aluminium	*aluminium*
das Gold	*gold*
das Kupfer	*copper*

(c) physical units

das Atom	*atom*
das Kilo	*kilogram(me)*

(d) letters of the alphabet

das ABC	*the ABC*
ein großes M	*a capital M*

(e) infinitives of verbs used as nouns

das Essen	*food, eating*
das Lernen	*learning*

(f) colours and languages

das Blau	*blue*
das Deutsch	*German*

(g) English -*ing* forms

das Meeting	*meeting*

(h) most "international" words

das Taxi	das Hotel
das Telefon	das Foto
das Café	das Restaurant

(i) most countries, regions, continents and towns

das schöne Irland	*beautiful Ireland*
das moderne Südamerika	*modern South America*
das neue Berlin	*the new Berlin*

Exceptions:

die Bretagne	*Brittany*	die Normandie	*Normandy*
die Pfalz	*the Palatinate*	die Schweiz	*Switzerland*
die Türkei	*Turkey*	die BRD	*Germany*

Tip: The following countries are plural:

die USA   *the USA*   die Niederlande   *the Netherlands*

Nouns — German Grammar

UNHELPFUL GENDERS OF NAMES OF HUMAN BEINGS

    das Fräulein   *young lady, "miss"*
    das Mädchen   *girl*
    das Mitglied   *member*
    die Person   *person*

COMPOUND WORDS

These take the gender and the plurals of the last part.

    Example: die Bushalte**stelle (n)**   *bus stop*
                    der Fahr**plan (-pläne)**   *timetable*
                    das Hallen**bad (-bäder)**   *indoor swimming pool*

LOAN WORDS FROM ENGLISH

Loan words from English are most often masculine, with neuter being the next most common. We have not given translations for these!

Masculine		Feminine		Neuter	
der Computer	der Stress	die Bar	die Email	das Baby	das Poster
der Hit	der Trend	die Party	die SMS	das Make-up	das Fax
der Jazz		die Show		das Handy *mobile phone*	
der Job		die Compact Disc		das Mountainbike	

NOUNS WITH MORE THAN ONE GENDER

Some nouns have more than one gender and, consequently, more than one meaning. Some of the common ones are listed here.

Masculine	Feminine	Neuter
der Band (Bände) *book*	die Band (s) *pop group*	das Band (Bänder) *ribbon*
der Messer (-) *surveyor/gauge*		das Messer (-) *knife*
der Pony (no pl) *fringe*		das Pony (s) *pony*
der See (n) *lake*	die See (no pl) *sea*	
	die Steuer (n) *tax*	das Steuer (-) *steering wheel*

PLURAL FORMS (PLURALFORMEN)

Many attempts have been made to describe the logic behind German plurals, most of them not totally satisfactory. We will confine our efforts to listing rules which always apply, and to giving the frequency of particular plural forms for those occasions when you have to guess. Unfortunately, the only way to make real headway in learning plural forms is to note them with each new word. There are no examples given here. It is far wiser to check individual words in a dictionary.

MASCULINE NOUNS (MASKULIN)

There are no hard-and-fast rules concerning the plurals of masculine nouns. The following guidelines might be helpful:

    (a)   the great majority of masculine nouns form their plural with **-e** or **"-e**
              The Umlaut is added in about half the cases.

German Grammar   Nouns

    (b)   the great majority of masculine nouns ending in **-el**, **-en** or **-er** form their plural with no change

    (c)   a small number of masculine nouns form their plural in **-er**, **-"er**, **-n** and **-en**

FEMININE NOUNS (FEMININ)

    (a)   over 90% of feminine nouns have the plural **-en** *or* **-n**

    (b)   only **die Mutter** and **die Tochter** have the plural **"**

    (c)   no feminine nouns have plurals with *no change* or **-"er**

NEUTER NOUNS (NEUTRUM)

    (a)   about 75% of neuter nouns have the plural **-e**

    (b)   most of the remainder have the plural **-"er**

LOAN WORDS FROM ENGLISH OR FRENCH

Most of these have plural in **-s**

DECLENSION OF NOUNS (DEKLINATION DER SUBSTANTIVE)

SPELLING CHANGES

There are slight spelling changes in German nouns in the following cases:

    (a)   In the Genitive singular, masculine and neuter nouns add an **-s**, or, if they only have one syllable, they add **-es**.

                Example: trotz des schlechten Wetter**s**
                            während des Tag**es**

    (b)   In the Dative plural for all genders, an **-n** is added if there is not one there already, or unless the plural ends in **-s**.

                Example: mit den Lehrer**n**

WEAK NOUNS (REGELMÄßIGE SUBSTANTIVE)

These nouns are slightly irregular.
They are **masculine** with the exception of 'das Herz'.

    (a)   The majority have **-en** throughout the plural and in all cases of the singular except the Nominative. They do not have an **-s** in the Genitive singular.

                Example:

	Singular	Plural
Nominative	der Junge	die Jungen
Accusative	den Jungen	die Jungen
Genitive	des Jungen	der Jungen
Dative	dem Jungen	den Jungen
Nominative	der Mensch	die Menschen
Accusative	den Menschen	die Menschen
Genitive	des Menschen	der Menschen
Dative	dem Menschen	den Menschen

Weak nouns include the following categories of nouns:

(i) Those masculine nouns ending in **-e** in the Nominative singular, which is how they are listed in the dictionary (except **der Käse** and those in (b) below).

These include:

der Affe	*monkey*
der Franzose	*Frenchman*

(ii) Some native masculine nouns not ending in **-e** in the Nominative singular:

These include:

der Herr	*gentleman*
der Mensch	*human being*
der Nachbar	*neighbour*
der Bauer	*farmer*
der Fotograf	*photographer*

(iii) Foreign masculine nouns ending in:
-and, -ant, aph, -arch, -at, -aut, -ent, -et, -ist, -krat -log, -nom, -on

These include:

der Polizist	*policeman*
der Student	*(university) student*
der Astronaut	*astronaut*
der Automat	*slot machine, robot*
der Demokrat	*democrat*
der Komet	*comet*
der Monarch	*monarch*

(iv) Some other foreign masculine nouns:

These include:

der Kamarad	*friend, comrade*
der Katholik	*Catholic*

(b) The following masculine nouns also behave like Junge in (a), except that they add an **-s** in the Genitive singular:

der Name	*name*
der Friede	*peace*
der Glaube	*belief*

Example: des Namens

(c) **Das Herz** has a unique pattern:

	Singular	Plural
Nominative:	das Herz	die Her**zen**
Accusative:	das Herz	die Her**zen**
Genitive:	des Herz**ens**	der Her**zen**
Dative:	dem Her**zen**	den Her**zen**

German Grammar   *Numbers*

NUMBERS (ZAHLEN)

CARDINAL NUMBERS (KARDINALZAHLEN)

0	null	10	zehn
1	eins	11	elf
2	zwei	12	zwölf
3	drei	13	dreizehn
4	vier	14	vierzehn
5	fünf	15	fünfzehn
6	sechs	16	sechzehn†
7	sieben	17	siebzehn†
8	acht	18	achtzehn
9	neun	19	neunzehn

20	zwanzig
21	einundzwanzig† (*Note the* **s** *has been dropped*)
22	zweiundzwanzig, etc

30	dreißig†
40	vierzig
50	fünfzig
60	sechzig†
70	siebzig†
80	achtzig
90	neunzig

100	hundert
101	hunderteins
102	hundertzwei
141	hunderteinundvierzig
200	zweihundert
999	neunhundertneunundneunzig
1000	tausend
1003	tausenddrei
1100	tausendeinhundert/elfhundert/eintausendeinhundert
1991	neunzehnhunderteinundneunzig
2006	zweitausendsechs
2007	zweitausendsieben
321 456	dreihunderteinundzwanzigtausendvierhundertsechsundfünfzig

1 000 000	eine Million (*spaces every 3 digits, no commas*)
56 500 200	sechsundfünfzig Millionen fünfhunderttausendzweihundert (*new word after* Millionen)
1 000 000 000	eine Milliarde
2 000 000 000	zwei Milliarden

Tip: † Beware the slightly unexpected spelling of these numbers

Numbers   *German Grammar*

CARDINAL NUMBERS: THE FINER POINTS

(a)   Years are usually stated in hundreds.
So 1992 = neunzehnhundertzweiundneunzig

(b)   Complex numbers are almost never written out in full: using figures is much clearer.

(c)   7 is usually written with a bar, to distinguish it from 1.

(d)   Where there is any danger of confusion, *zwo* is used instead of *zwei*. It is often heard in public announcements, and on the telephone.

(e)   Longer numbers - such as telephone numbers after dialling codes - are written and read in pairs. So 02531/ 65 54 08 is pronounced as: Null zwo fünf drei eins, fünfundsechzig vierundfünfzig null acht.

(f)   Cardinal numbers can be used as nouns, particularly when discussing school grades.

        Example: Ich habe eine Eins in Mathe
                             I have a 1 in maths

ORDINAL NUMBERS - FORMATION (ORDINALZAHLEN)

Nearly all ordinal numbers are formed as follows:

(a)   2nd - 19th add **-te** to the cardinal number. However the following four ordinal numbers and their compounds have variations to the rule.

der **erste** Mai	1st *May*
der **dritte** Mai	3rd *May*
der **siebte** Mai	7th *May*
der **achte** Mai	8th *May*

Unless they are immediately followed by a noun, they are written with a capital letter.

Example: der Zweite *the 2nd*, der siebzehnte Mai *17th May*

(b)   20th and upwards add **-ste** to the cardinal number. The same rule about capital letters as in (a) applies.

Example: der Dreißig**ste**	*the 30th*
der Tausend**ste**	*the 1000th*
der Dreiundvierzig**ste**	*the 43rd*
der hundert**ste** Geburtstag	*the 100th birthday*
das hunderttausend**ste** Ei	*the $100,000^{th}$ egg*

However, if the number above 20 ends with part of the compound derived from a number less than 20, the endings in (a) apply.

> Example: der hundert**zweite** Läufer   *the 102nd runner*
> der tausend**erste** Nacht   *the 1001st night*
> der Dreihundertsiebzehnte   *the 317th*

ORDINAL NUMBERS - USAGE

Ordinal numbers present few problems.

(a) They are in fact adjectives, and take the usual endings.

(b) In writing, it is preferable to write them as numerals, which **must** have a full stop.

> Example: am 20. 2. (pronounced: am zwanzigsten zweiten)
> *on the twentieth of the second*
> der 101. Versuch
> *the 101st attempt*

FRACTIONS (BRUCHZAHLEN)

(a) Apart from "half", most fractions are formed by adding **-l** to the ordinal number.

> Example: ein Drittel (-)   *a third*
> ein Sechstel (-)   *a sixth*

(b) "Half" can be translated either by the noun *die Hälfte* or by the adjective *halb*.

> Example:
> die Hälfte   Ich habe nur **die Hälfte** von meiner Hausaufgabe gemacht
> *I have only done half of my homework*
>
> halb   Ich aß einen **halben** Apfel
> *I ate half an apple*

(c) One and a half is **eineinhalb**.
The same pattern continues with **zweieinhalb, dreieinhalb,** *etc*.
Anderthalb is a common alternative form of **eineinhalb**.

(d) Germans write decimals with a comma and not a point.

> Example: Fünf durch zwei ergibt 2,5   (pronounced: zwei Komma fünf)
> *Five divided by two is 2.5*

PREPOSITIONS (PRÄPOSITIONEN)

Prepositions are words which are used to show a relationship between one noun and another. This word often shows the position of one thing in relation to another. Prepositions in German are followed by different cases. For most prepositions, it is merely a matter of knowing which one they "take". For example, **von** takes the Dative. However, there are a few common prepositions which take either Accusative or Dative according to their meaning.

PREPOSITIONS WHICH ALWAYS TAKE THE ACCUSATIVE
(PRÄPOSITIONEN MIT DEM AKKUSATIV)

bis	*as far as; until*
durch	*through; throughout*
für	*for*
gegen	*against; towards; about*
ohne	*without*
um	*at + clock times; round; about; concerning;*
pro	*per*
wider	*against*

Example: **für** meinen Vater — *for my father*
durch die Aula — *through the school hall*

PREPOSITIONS WHICH ALWAYS TAKE THE DATIVE
(PRÄPOSITIONEN MIT DEM DATIV)

aus	*out of; made of*
außer	*except for; out of (use)*
bei	*by; at; at the house of; on the occasion of*
gegenüber†	*opposite; compared with; in relation to; towards*
mit	*with; by*
nach	*to; towards; after + time; according to*
seit	*since; for (uses a more recent tense than in English)*
von	*from; of*
zu	*to; at; for; as; towards; at + price*

† may come before or after the noun

Example: **mit** meinem Freund — *with my (boy)friend*
seit zwei Jahren — *for two years*
der Kirche **gegenüber** — *opposite the church*

Tips:
- It is tempting to think both **aus** and **zu** might take the Accusative because they imply motion (see below). They **NEVER** take the Accusative.
- Remember that most nouns add an **-n** in the Dative plural if they do not already have one. This is often forgotten.

Example: Ich sehe meine alten Freunde mit meinen neuen Freunde**n**

PREPOSITIONS WHICH TAKE EITHER ACCUSATIVE OR DATIVE
(PRÄPOSITIONEN MIT DEM AKKUSATIV ODER DATIV)

Ten common prepositions can take either Accusative or Dative. These can best be learnt in related groups.

in	*in; into; inside*
an	*on (the side of); onto; at; of*
auf	*on (top of); at; in*
hinter (usually + Dat)	*behind*
vor (usually + Dat)	*in front of; before*
über	*over; about; more than*
unter (usually + Dat)	*under; below; among*
neben (usually + Dat)	*next to*
zwischen (usually + Dat)	*between*
entlang† (usually + Acc)	*along*

† follows the noun

When deciding which case to use after these prepositions, remember that two basic rules apply to the majority of instances.

(a) If the preposition is about position, then the Dative is used. If it is about motion towards, then the Accusative is used. It may be helpful to memorise this couplet:

Dative is for place of rest
Accusative for motion's best

Example: Ich gehe **in die** Schule   (in + Accusative - motion)
I go to school
Ich arbeite **in der** Schule   (in + Dative - position)
I work in school

Verbs of arriving, appearing and disappearing are usually used in conjunction with a Dative.

Example: Ich komme um 8 Uhr 30 **in der Schule** an
I arrive at school at 8.30

Prepositions — German Grammar

b) If the preposition is used in a figurative sense (something of which you could not make a model), it often takes the Accusative.

Example: Ursula wartet **auf den Bus**
Ursula is waiting for the bus
Ich freue mich **auf deinen nächsten Brief**
I am looking forward to your next letter
Ich denke **an dich**
I'm thinking of you
Auf Ihr Wohl!
Cheers! To your good health!

Tip: Although the rules given above *can* apply to most of the Accusative/Dative prepositions, in practice the majority of them are most frequently found with the cases we have given in brackets. The ones which most often require thinking about are **an, auf, in** and **über**. Watch out for verbs of movement such as **gehen, fahren** or **kommen** in the sentence, when an accusative will most probably be required with the preposition.

PREPOSITIONS WHICH TAKE THE GENITIVE (PRÄPOSITIONEN MIT DEM GENITIV)

These are listed with the three most common ones first, then related pairs.

trotz	*despite, in spite of*
während	*during*
wegen	*because of*
außerhalb	*outside (of)*
innerhalb	*within*
statt	*instead of*
anstatt	*instead of*

Example: **während** der Ferien *during the holidays*
trotz der Hitze *despite the heat*

Tip: Remember that masculine and neuter nouns add an **-s** in the Genitive singular.

Example: **wegen** des schlechten Wetter**s**
because of the bad weather

PRONOUNS (PRONOMEN)

Pronouns take the place of a noun, often to avoid repetition. The case of the pronoun is determined by its task in the sentence.

PERSONAL PRONOUNS (PERSONALPRONOMEN)

Singular   **Plural**

Nominative

ich	*I*		wir	*we*
du	*you (singular, familiar)*		ihr	*you (plural, familiar)*
Sie	*you (singular, formal)*		Sie	*you (plural, formal)*
er	*he* or *it*		sie	*they*
sie	*she* or *it*			
es	*it*			
man	*one*			

Accusative

mich	*me*		uns	*us*
dich	*you (singular, familiar)*		euch	*you (plural, familiar)*
Sie	*you (singular, formal)*		Sie	*you (plural, formal)*
ihn	*him* or *it*		sie	*them*
sie	*her* or *it*			
es	*it*			
einen	*one*			

Dative

mir	*to me*		uns	*to us*
dir	*to you (singular, familiar)*	euch		*to you (plural, familiar)*
Ihnen	*to you (singular, formal)*	Ihnen		*to you (plural, formal)*
ihm	*to him* or *to it*	ihnen		*to them*
ihr	*to her* or *to it*			
ihm	*to it*			
einem	*to one*			

Pronouns   *German Grammar*

REFLEXIVE PRONOUNS (REFLEXIVPRONOMEN)

(a)   The Accusative reflexive pronouns are as in the example below:

ich wasche **mich**	*I wash myself*
du wäschst **dich**	*you wash yourself*
Sie waschen **sich**	*you wash yourself*
er wäscht **sich**	*he washes himself*
sie wäscht **sich**	*she washes herself*
es wäscht **sich**	*it washes itself*
man wäscht **sich**	*one washes oneself*
Sam wäscht **sich**	*Sam washes himself/herself*
wir waschen **uns**	*we wash ourselves*
ihr wascht **euch**	*you wash yourselves*
Sie waschen **sich**	*you wash yourselves*
sie waschen **sich**	*they wash themselves*
die Kinder waschen **sich**	*the children wash themselves*

(b)   The Dative reflexive pronouns are as follows:

ich wasche **mir** die Hände	*I wash my hands*
du wäschst **dir** die Hände	*you wash your hands*
Sie waschen **sich** die Hände	*you wash your hands*
er wäscht **sich** die Hände	*he washes his hands*
sie wäscht **sich** die Hände	*she washes her hands*
es wäscht **sich** die Hände	*it washes its hands*
man wäscht **sich** die Hände	*one washes one's hands*
Sam wäscht **sich** die Hände	*Sam washes his/her hands*
wir waschen **uns** die Hände	*we wash our hands*
ihr wascht **euch** die Hände	*you wash your hands*
Sie waschen **sich** die Hände	*you wash your hands*
sie waschen **sich** die Hände	*they wash their hands*
die Kinder waschen **sich** die Hände	*the children wash their hands*

Tip: The Accusative and Dative Reflexive Pronouns are only different after **ich** and **du**.

DU or SIE?

Germans are very concerned to use the correct form for "you". Getting it wrong is impolite. The following are the main rules concerning choice of "you":

(a)   **du/dich/dir/dein** is used for speaking to a child (up to about 15) or an animal, and between children, students, relatives and close friends.

(b)   **ihr/euch/euch/euer** (**euer** drops the second **e** if followed by an **e** - thus **eure**) is used to address a group of two or more people in which at least some would be addressed as **du**.

(c)   **Sie/Sie/Ihnen/Ihr** is used on all other occasions, and particularly between adult strangers.

German Grammar *Pronouns*

ER, SIE and ES

(a) For native speakers of English, it is important to remember that "it" may refer to a masculine or feminine noun in German, and that **er** or **sie** may be needed in preference to **es**, which is reserved for neuter nouns in the nominative or accusative. **Er** and **sie** do not refer solely to biological gender. See NOUNS, pages 25-30.

    Example: Hier ist die Tasche. Ich habe **sie** gestern gekauft
                          Here is the bag. I bought it yesterday
                          Hier ist der neue Stuhl. Ich habe **ihn** gestern bekommen
                          Here is the new chair. I got it yesterday.

(b) There is occasional confusion between biological and grammatical gender, particularly with **das Fräulein** and **das Mädchen**. They can be referred to as either **es** or **sie**.

(c) **es** is never used after a preposition. Instead the preposition has the prefix **da(r)** attached to give **damit, darauf,** *etc.*

    Example: Endlich kommt der Zug an. Wir haben eine Stunde **darauf** gewartet
                          Here is the train at last. We've been waiting for it for an hour

RELATIVE PRONOUNS (RELATIVPRONOMEN)

Relative pronouns are used to translate the English *who, whom, whose, which* or *that*. It is important to know how to check whether *that* is actually a relative pronoun or best translated by **dass**. The test is this: if *that* can be replaced by *who* or *which* without changing the meaning, it is a relative pronoun. If you have made nonsense by the replacement, use **dass**.

    Example: This is the Volkswagen **that** I bought
                          Replace *that* with *which*:
                          This is the Volkswagen **which** I bought
                          This makes sense, so the original *that* is a relative pronoun.

                          I think **that** they should come with you
                          Replace *that* with *which*:
                          I think **which** they should come with you
                          This is nonsense, so *that* must be **dass**.

Tip: **dass** often follows a verb, for example *Ich glaube, dass* ...

A further complication is that the relative pronoun is often missed out in English, in such sentences as: Here is the book I saw in town
                     = Here is the book **which** I saw in town
                       Hier ist das Buch, **das** ich in der Stadt gesehen habe

The relative pronoun is NEVER omitted in German.

(a) **Form of the Relative Pronoun**

	Masc	Fem	Neuter	Plural	Meaning
Nominative	der	die	das	die	*who, which, that*
Accusative	den	die	das	die	*who(m), which, that*
Genitive	dessen	deren	dessen	deren	*whose, of which*
Dative	dem	der	dem	denen	*to whom, to which*

(b) **Agreement**

The relative pronoun agrees using the following rules:
Look BACK for **gender** (masculine, feminine or neuter) and **number** (singular or plural).
Look FORWARD for **case**.

The gender and number must be the gender and number of the noun to which the relative pronoun refers, as is shown by these relative pronouns in the Genitive case.

> Example: Mein Bruder, **dessen** ...   *my brother, whose* ... (masc sing)
> Meine Schwester, **deren** ...   *my sister, whose* ... (fem sing)
> Meine Kinder, **deren** ...   *my children, whose* ... (plural)
>
> Der Junge, **dessen** Mutter krank war, half seinem Vater jeden Tag
> *The boy **whose** mother was ill helped his father every day*

(c) **Case**

If the relative pronoun is the subject and the **Nominative** case is required, there will be nothing in English between the relative pronoun and the verb (who teaches).

> Example: Herr Braun ist der Lehrer, **der** Sport unterrichtet
> *Herr Braun is the teacher **who/that teaches** games*

If it is the object and the **Accusative** case is required, there will be a noun or pronoun between the relative pronoun and the verb in English (who/whom I saw).

> Example: Der Mann, **den** ich in der Schule sah, war mir fremd
> *The man **(that/who/whom)** I saw in school was a stranger to me*

Sometimes there may be a preposition before the relative pronoun.
The preposition will then determine which case to use:

> Example: **with whom - mit + Dative**
>
> Die Kinder, **mit denen** wir plauderten, kamen aus Düsseldorf
> *The children **with whom** we were chatting came from Düsseldorf*
> *The children **(who)** we were chatting **with** came from Düsseldorf*

(d) After **alles, nichts, etwas,** and the less frequently found **einiges, Folgendes, manches** and **vieles, was** is always the relative pronoun.

   Example: Alles, **was** ich esse, ist gesund
   Everything I eat is healthy

(e) Note how **das, was** is used:

   Example: Wir haben nur **das, was** wir gepackt haben
   We only have what we have packed (that which we have packed)

Tip: Remember that the relative pronoun sends the verb to the end of the clause, and has a comma in front of it.

INTERROGATIVE PRONOUNS (INTERROGATIVPRONOMEN)

These are question words which change according to case. The case is determined by their function in the sentence.

(a) *who?* changes as follows:

Nominative	wer?	*who?*
Accusative	wen?	*who(m)?*
Genitive	wessen?	*whose?*
Dative	wem?	*to whom?*

   Example: **Wessen** Foto ist das?
   ***Whose** photo is that?*
   Wen hast du in Mathe?
   ***Who(m)** do you have for Maths?*

(b) Where *what* is used as a question word and is combined with a preposition, the preposition has **wo(r)-** added to the front of it. A bonus of this arrangement is that you don't have to work out which case it should be!

   Example: **Womit** schreibst du, und **worauf**?
   *What are you writing **with**, and **on**?*

(c) **Welcher** *which* changes as follows:

	Masculine	Feminine	Neuter	Plural	Meaning
Nominative	welcher	welche	welches	welche	*which*
Accusative	welchen	welche	welches	welche	*which*
Genitive	welches	welcher	welches	welcher	*of which*
Dative	welchem	welcher	welchem	welchen	*to which*

Welcher agrees with the noun to which it refers.

> Example: Welch**es** Buch soll ich kaufen?
> *Which book should I buy?*

Welcher is also used as a slightly more formal alternative to the standard relative pronoun.

> Example: Der Schuldirektor, welch**er** seit Jahren gegen weiße Socken gewesen ist, hat sie plötzlich erlaubt
> *The Headteacher, **who** had been against white socks for years, suddenly allowed them*

DEMONSTRATIVE PRONOUNS (DEMONSTRATIVPRONOMEN)

(a) These agree with the noun to which they refer, and decline like this:

	Masculine	**Feminine**	**Neuter**	**Plural**
Nominative	dies**er**	dies**e**	dies**es**	dies**e**
Accusative	dies**en**	dies**e**	dies**es**	dies**e**
Genitive	dies**es**	dies**er**	dies**es**	dies**er**
Dative	dies**em**	dies**er**	dies**em**	dies**en**

Others which follow this pattern are:
- dieser — *this*
- jener — *that*
- jeder — *each/every*
- solcher — *such a, like this*

(b) **der** + something can be combined to make a demonstrative, for example **derjenige, dieselbe, dasselbe**. Both parts of these compounds have to agree in case, number and gender. The first part behaves like **der, die, das** in Table 1 (page 6), and the second part takes the adjective endings from Table 1.

> Example: **Diejenigen**, die zu **derselben** Zeit mit **demselben** Bus nach Neustrelitz fahren wollten, waren alle Musiker
> *Those who wanted to travel to Neustrelitz on the same bus at the same time were all musicians*

(c) Adjectives which follow Demonstratives have endings from Table 1 (page 6).

> Example: Dies**er** rot**e** Wagen gehört meiner Nachbarin
> *This red car belongs to my neighbour*

SPELLING AND PUNCTUATION
(RECHTSCHREIBUNG UND ZEICHENSETZUNG)

SPELLING (RECHTSCHREIBUNG)

(a) The Umlaut (Der Umlaut)

A common mistake is **Umlaut** blindness. The English-speaking learner (suffering from **Umlaut** deafness) assumes that they are mere decoration and have no significance. In fact they often convey significant subtleties of meaning, as can be seen by checking out the sections on CONDITIONAL, COMPARISONS and NOUNS. So an **Umlaut** mistake should be treated as a serious one.

Tip: Remember schon = *already* and schön = *beautiful*.

(b) ss or ß?

As a result of the German Spelling Reform of 1998, after a short vowel **ß** has been replaced by **ss**.   Example: dass, ich muss, ein bisschen
It is best to learn whether a word is spelt with **ss** or **ß** when you come across it for the first time.

PUNCTUATION (ZEICHENSETZUNG)

Punctuation in English often conveys meaning and even indicates where to breathe.
In German it follows stricter rules.

(a) Capital Letters (Großbuchstaben)

These are used:

- at the start of sentences
- for all nouns, wherever they occur
- for the "polite" personal pronouns except **sich**, and the possessives which go with them (**Sie, Sie, Ihnen, Ihr**)
- in titles of films, books, etc

They are NOT used for nationalities when these are adjectives or adverbs, but they are used where nationalities are nouns.

> Example: Der **deutsche** Bus hatte einen Slogan auf **Englisch**
> *The German bus had a slogan in English*

(b) Commas (Kommas)

These are used:

- in lists, except just before the **und**

> Example: Er hatte zwei Autos**,** ein Fahrrad und ein Motorrad
> *He had two cars, a bicycle and a motorbike*

Spelling and Punctuation — German Grammar

- where there are two main clauses linked by a co-ordinating conjunction when the subject is changed or repeated

    Example: Die Hauptstadt von Frankreich ist Paris, und die Hauptstadt von Deutschland ist Berlin
    The capital of France is Paris and the capital of Germany is Berlin

- to separate a subordinate clause from the main clause

    Example: Ich fahre mit dem Bus zur Schule, wenn es regnet
    I come to school by bus when it is raining
    Wenn es regnet, fahre ich mit dem Bus zur Schule
    When it is raining I come to school by bus

The second example shows the common word order sequence **verb - comma - verb**.

However, no comma is used if the subordinate clause is simply a 2-word clause consisting of **zu** + infinitive

    Example: Ich hatte Lust zu lernen   *I wanted to learn*

(c) Exclamation marks (Ausrufezeichen)

These are used:

- after commands (even whispered ones!)

    Example: Setzt euch!   *Sit down*

- after exclamations

    Example: Ach!   *Oh!*

- often after the opening of a letter

    Example: Liebe Frau Krechel!   *Dear Frau Krechel,*
              Wie geht es Ihnen?   *How are you?*

This usage is rapidly being replaced by a more modern version using a comma.

    Liebe Frau Krechel,
        wie geht es Ihnen?

The **w** on **wie** does NOT have a capital letter in this version.

(d) Direct Speech (Direkte Rede)

This is written as follows:

    Ich fragte: „Wo wohnst du?"

WORD ORDER (WORTSTELLUNG)

The order of certain groups of words in German follows a set of rules.

VERBS (VERBEN)

(a) In a simple sentence, the verb is the second idea. It may come after the subject, after another idea, or after a subordinate clause. In compound tenses such as the perfect tense, the auxiliary (**haben** or **sein**) occupies the position of second idea in the sentence, while the past participle is at the end of the sentence. The rest of the sentence is sandwiched between the two.
Our preference is to call this rule the "1 - 2 - 3 rule".

Example:

	VERB		
1st idea	2nd idea	3rd idea	
Ich	gehe	am Samstag in die Stadt	
Am Samstag	gehe	ich in die Stadt	
In die Stadt	gehe	ich am Samstag	
I am going to town on Saturday			
1st idea	2nd idea	3rd idea	
Wenn es sonnig ist,	gehe	ich in die Stadt	
If it is sunny I'll go into town			
1st idea	2nd idea	3rd idea	Past Participle
Ich	bin	in die Stadt	gegangen
I went into town			
Ich	habe	ein Buch	gekauft
I bought a book			

Tip: If you start a sentence with something other than the subject it does not change the fundamental meaning. But if you put something other than the subject at the start of a sentence then that something is often being emphasised.

(b) If two sentences are joined by a **co-ordinating conjunction** such as **und, aber** or **oder**, the conjunction does **not** count in the word order. The resulting sentence behaves like two separate sentences joined by an invisible conjunction.

Example: Ich **mag** Mathe aber ich **mag** lieber Chemie
I like Maths but I prefer Chemistry

(c) If a clause is joined to the rest of the sentence by a **subordinating conjunction**, the verb (or the auxiliary) goes to the end of that clause. The past participle or infinitive comes before the auxiliary.

Example: Renate weiß, dass sie zu spät abgefahren **ist**
Renate knows that she has set off too late
Ich habe keine Ahnung, wann sie ankommen **wird**
I have no idea when she will arrive
Wenn es um 8 Uhr **regnet,** fahre ich mit dem Bus zur Schule
If it is raining at 8 o'clock I travel to school by bus

Word Order — German Grammar

(d) In the main clause, when there is only one verb and it is separable, the two parts of the separable verb are separated and the prefix becomes the last word in the sentence.

> Example: Ich **sehe** heute abend **fern**   *I'm watching TV tonight*

If the separable verb is the second verb and is in the infinitive form, it stays together and is the last word in the sentence.

> Example: Ich darf nicht **fernsehen**   *I'm not allowed to watch TV*

In a subordinate clause the two parts of a separable verb are joined together.

> Example: Als ich **ankam**   *When I arrived*
> als er **angekommen ist**   *when he arrived*

(e) Modal verbs behave as the auxiliary verbs **haben** and **sein**. Thus they are the second idea in a main clause and the infinitive goes to the end of the sentence. In a subordinate clause the modal verb is the last word and the infinitive comes before it.

> Example: Ich **kann** gut **schwimmen**   *I can swim well*
> weil ich **schwimmen kann**   *because I can swim*

(f) In questions with a question word the verb comes second.

> Example: Wann **kommt** der Bus an?   *When does the bus arrive?*

In any other question the verb comes first.

> Example: **Kommt** er um 8 Uhr an?   *Is he arriving at 8 o'clock?*

TIME, MANNER, PLACE

In German, time usually comes as early as possible in a sentence. This is more or less the opposite to common English usage.

(a) The order of adverbs or adverbial phrases which are next to each other is usually **time** (when) before **manner** (how) before **place** (where).

> | | Time | Manner | Place |
> |----------|---------------|--------------|---------------|
> | Example: Ich fahre | jeden Samstag | mit dem Wagen | nach Worcester |
> | *I go* | *every Saturday* | *by car* | *to Worcester* |
>
> *I go to Worcester by car every Saturday*

German Grammar — Word Order

(b) If there is more than one expression of a particular type, the more general one comes before the less general, more specific one.

	Time (general)	Time (more specific)
Example: Peter ruft seine Mutter	**jeden Tag**	**um 2 Uhr an**
Peter phones his mother	*every day*	*at 2 o'clock*

DATIVE AND ACCUSATIVE (DATIV UND AKKUSATIV)

The order of Dative and Accusative objects in German follows fixed rules.

(a) If the Dative and the Accusative are *both* nouns, the Dative comes first.

	Dative	**Accusative**
Example: Ich gebe	**dem Mann**	**einen Bleistift**
I give	*the man*	*a pencil*

(b) If the Dative and the Accusative are *both* pronouns, the Accusative comes first.

	Accusative	**Dative**
Example: Ich gebe	**es**	**ihr**
I give	*it*	*(to) her*

Tip: (a) and (b) can be remembered by the mnemonic **P A D D A N**
(With **P**ronouns: **A**ccusative then **D**ative; **D**ative then **A**ccusative with **N**ouns)

(c) If one is a pronoun and the other is a noun, the pronoun comes first, no matter which case it is in.

	Pronoun	**Noun**
Example: Ich gebe	**es**	**der Dame**
I give	*it*	*to the lady*
	Pronoun	**Noun**
Ich gebe	**ihr**	**den Bleistift**
I give	*her*	*the pencil*

VERBS (VERBEN)

GENERAL INFORMATION

A verb is a "doing word". It conveys information about what is done, who or what does it, and when the action took place, takes place, or will take place.

PERSONS (PERSONEN)

The form of all verbs in German is determined in part by the "subject". This is generally the person or thing which performs the action of the verb. (But see PASSIVE, pages 57-61)

The subject can be one of three possible "persons".

The first person is used when the speaker performs the action of the verb:
  ich, wir

The second person is used when the person being spoken to performs the action of the verb: **du, Sie, ihr**

The third person is used when neither the speaker nor the person being spoken to is performing the action of the verb. The action is being performed by someone else:
  er, sie (= she), **Sam, es, man, sie** (= they), **die Kinder, Herr und Frau Schmidt**

FORMS OF GERMAN VERBS (FORMEN DES DEUTSCHEN VERBS)

When a verb is listed in a dictionary or word list, it is given in the **Infinitive**.
  Example: wohnen   *to live*
                   gehen   *to go, to walk*

The infinitive will normally be the starting point in describing how tenses are formed.

The verb indicates by its tense **when** the action described occurs, has occurred or will occur. The main tenses and their uses are given below.

REGULAR (WEAK), IRREGULAR (STRONG) AND MIXED VERBS
(SCHWACHE, STARKE UND GEMISCHTE VERBEN)

There are two sorts of verbs in German:

(a)   **Regular**, which follow a rule. Regular verbs are often called **weak** verbs in German (because they do not have a "mind of their own").

(b)   **Irregular**, which do not always follow a rule and therefore have to be learnt. Irregular German verbs are often called **strong** verbs (because they are "strong-minded").

The majority of verbs in any dictionary are regular (weak). However, in any piece of German of any length there will probably be a majority of irregular (strong) verbs, because they often express common actions.

German Grammar *Verbs*

Mixed verbs are often mentioned in some dictionaries and grammars. These verbs are irregular, but share some of the characteristics of regular (weak) verbs. While that is true, the fact remains that they are still irregular, and need to be learnt like irregular (strong) verbs. We have included them in the irregular verb table. (see page 84)

PRESENT TENSE (DAS PRÄSENS)

It is used for
- actions which are happening now
- actions which happen regularly
- actions which will happen in the future.

Example: Ich **wohne** in Malvern, ich **gehe** nach Hause

Therefore can mean:
ich gehe nach Hause
I am going home (now)
I go home (regularly)
I am going home (at some point in the future)

Note that the addition of **nicht** creates an additional set of meanings in English.

Therefore can mean:
as well as:
ich gehe nicht nach Hause
I do not go home
I am not going home

The Present tense is formed as follows:

(a) **Regular (weak) verbs (Schwache Verben)**

Remove **-en** from the infinitive and add the following endings:

		Singular			Plural	
1st person	ich		-e	wir		-en
2nd person	du		-st	ihr		-t
	Sie		-en	Sie		-en
3rd person	er/sie/es/man/Sam		-t	sie/die Kinder		-en

Example:
ich wohne	*I live, I am living, I do live*
du wohnst	*you live, you are living, you do live*
Sie wohnen	*you live, you are living, you do live*
er/sie/es/man wohnt	*he/she/it/one lives, is living, does live*
Sam wohnt	*Sam lives, Sam is living, Sam does live*
wir wohnen	*we live, we are living, we do live*
ihr wohnt	*you live, you are living, you do live*
Sie wohnen	*you live, you are living, you do live*
sie wohnen	*they live, they are living, they do live*
die Kinder wohnen	*the children live, are living, do live*

(b)   **Irregular (strong) verbs (Starke Verben)**

Check the irregular verb table (see page 84). If there is no vowel change listed and shown in **bold** in the verb table under "3rd person Present", then the verb behaves in the same way as regular (weak) verbs in the present tense. If there is a vowel change, it affects the **du** and **er/sie/es/man** forms only. The endings are the same as for regular (weak) verbs.

Example without a vowel change:

ich gehe	*I go, I am going, I do go*
du gehst	*you go, you are going, you do go*
Sie gehen	*you go, you are going, you do go*
er/sie/es/man geht	*he/she/it/one goes, is going, does go*
Sam geht	*Sam goes, is going, does go*
wir gehen	*we go, we are going, we do go*
ihr geht	*you go, you are going, you do go*
Sie gehen	*you go, you are going, you do go*
sie gehen	*they go, they are going, they do go*
die Kinder gehen	*the children go, are going, do go*

Example with a vowel change:

ich sehe	*I see, I am seeing, I do see*
du siehst	*you see, you are seeing, you do see*
Sie sehen	*you see, you are seeing, you do see*
er/sie/es/man sieht	*he/she/it/one sees, is seeing, does see*
Sam sieht	*Sam sees, is seeing, does see*
wir sehen	*we see, we are seeing, we do see*
ihr seht	*you see, you are seeing, you do see*
Sie sehen	*you see, you are seeing, you do see*
sie sehen	*they see, they are seeing, they do see*
die Kinder sehen	*the children see, are seeing, do see*

Verbs (irregular or regular) whose infinitives end in **-den, -ten, -chnen, -cknen, -dnen, -fnen, -gnen**, or **-tnen** take the endings **-est** and **-et** in the second and third person singular and the second person plural **ihr** as the extra **e** makes pronunciation easier.

Example: du arbei**test**, er öff**net**, ihr wer**det**

The Present tense of **sein** is:

ich bin, du bist, Sie sind, er/sie/es/man ist, wir sind, ihr seid, Sie sind, sie sind

Wissen has the form **ich weiß**. For modal verbs see page 65.

Tips:
- Remember that the Present tense means not only *I go* but also *I am going* and *I do (not) go*. You must resist the temptation to translate the separate parts of *I am going* into German - it's WRONG!
- The Present tense is quite often used with an adverb of time to give a future meaning:

    Ich **fliege** morgen nach Wien
    I am flying to Vienna tomorrow

German Grammar *Verbs*

FUTURE TENSE (DAS FUTUR)

This is the tense used for actions or events which will take place in the future, often at a time which is quite distant from the present moment.

Example:
    Ich **werde** in Malvern **wohnen**   *I shall (will) live in Malvern*
                                               I shall (will) be living in Malvern
    Ich **werde** nach Hause **gehen**   *I shall (will) go home*
                                               I shall (will) be going home

The Future is formed in the same way for both regular (weak) and irregular (strong) verbs. The verb is in two parts, the Present tense of **werden** and, at the end of the clause or sentence, the *infinitive* of the verb in question.

(a) **Regular (weak) verbs**

wohnen
ich werde in Malvern wohnen	*I shall/will live, be living in Malvern*
du wirst in Malvern wohnen	*you will live, be living in Malvern*
Sie werden in Malvern wohnen	*you will live, be living in Malvern*
er/sie/es/man wird in York wohnen	*he/she/it/one will live, be living in York*
Sam wird in Malvern wohnen	*Sam will live, be living in Malvern*
wir werden in Malvern wohnen	*we shall/will live, be living in Malvern*
ihr werdet in Malvern wohnen	*you will live, be living in Malvern*
Sie werden in Malvern wohnen	*you will live, be living in Malvern*
sie werden in Malvern wohnen	*they will live, be living in Malvern*
die Kinder werden in York wohnen	*the children will live, be living in York*

(b) **Irregular (strong) verbs**

gehen*
ich werde nach Hause gehen	*I shall/will go home, be going home*
du wirst nach Hause gehen	*you will go home, be going home*
Sie werden nach Hause gehen	*you will go home, be going home*
er/sie/es/man wird nach Hause gehen	*he/she/it/one will go home, be going home*
Sam wird nach Hause gehen	*Sam will go home, be going home*
wir werden nach Hause gehen	*we shall/will go home, be going home*
ihr werdet nach Hause gehen	*you will go home, be going home*
Sie werden nach Hause gehen	*you will go home, be going home*
sie werden nach Hause gehen	*they will go home, be going home*
die Kinder werden nach Hause gehen	*the children will go home, be going home*

Tip: **werden*** itself follows the same pattern, although the infinitive is not needed in such sentences as:

    Ich **werde** Busfahrer   *I shall become a bus driver*

Verbs   *German Grammar*

PERFECT TENSE (DAS PERFEKT)

The Perfect is the past tense most frequently used in speech, letters and other informal writing to talk about actions which are completed. It translates a variety of English past tenses.

Therefore   ich **habe** in Malvern **gewohnt**   ich **bin** nach Hause **gegangen**
can mean: *I lived in Malvern*   *I went home*
                   I was living in Malvern   *I was going home*
                   I have lived in Malvern   *I have gone home*
                   I have been living in Malvern   *I have been going home*

This tense is formed in two parts, with the Present tense of **haben** or **sein** and, at the end of the clause or sentence, the past participle of the verb. The Present tense of **haben** or **sein** is known as the **auxiliary** verb, although the German term **Hilfsverb** is perhaps clearer!

(a)   **Regular (weak) verbs**

Nearly all regular verbs, including reflexives, form the Perfect tense with **haben** as the auxiliary. See below: **haben or sein?** (page 54)

The past participle is usually formed by adding **ge-** as a prefix to the infinitive, removing the **-en** and replacing it with **-t**, as in: **wohnen** → **gewohnt**

If the infinitive ends in **-den, -ten, -chnen, -cknen, -dnen, -fnen, -gnen,** or **-tnen** (see Present tense, page 50), then an extra **-e** is added before the final **-t** to make the pronunciation easier, as in: **arbeiten** → **gearbeitet**

If the infinitive ends in **-ieren**, then no **ge-** prefix is added, as in: studiert, telefoniert

No **ge-** is added when the verb starts with a prefix which does not separate. These prefixes are: **be-, ent-, emp-, er-, ge-, miss-, ver-** and **zer-**, as in: besucht, verkauft

If the verb has a prefix which *does* separate, the *ge* is slipped in between the prefix and the past participle, as in: **ein**kaufen→ ein**ge**kauft.

Once the past participle has been formed, the only change in the verb is to the auxiliary.

        wohnen
            ich habe .... gewohnt   *I lived, have lived, have been living*
            du hast .... gewohnt   *you lived, have lived, have been living*
            Sie haben .... gewohnt   *you lived, have lived, have been living*
            er/sie/es/man hat ..... gewohnt   *he/she/it/one lived, has lived, has been living*
            Sam hat .... gewohnt   *Sam lived, has lived, has been living*
            wir haben .... gewohnt   *we lived, have lived, have been living*
            ihr habt .... gewohnt   *you lived, have lived, have been living*
            Sie haben .... gewohnt   *you lived, have lived, have been living*
            sie haben .... gewohnt   *they lived, have lived, have been living*
            die Kinder haben ..... gewohnt   *the children lived, have lived, have been living*

German Grammar — Verbs

(b) **Irregular (strong) and "mixed"**

While many of these verbs form the Perfect tense using **haben** as the auxiliary, a lot of them use **sein** as the auxiliary. See page 54, **haben or sein?**

Because these verbs are irregular, the only safe way to discover the past participle is to look the verb up in a verb table. If the verb you are looking for does not seem to be in the table, it is possible that it is a compound of another verb, with one of the prefixes: **be-, ent-, emp-, er-, ge-, miss-, ver-** or **zer-** on the front. For example, compounds like bekommen and ankommen* *sep* behave in a similar way to **kommen***.

Some dictionaries and glossaries list only the vowel changes. So **sehen** would appear as **sehen (ie,a,e)**. The first vowel in the brackets is the third person singular Present. The second one is the Imperfect, and the final vowel is the past participle vowel.

    Example: er sieht   er sah   er hat gesehen

Irregular verbs often have a past participle which ends in **-en (fahren → gefahren)**. It may or may not have a different main vowel from the infinitive:

    lesen → gelesen   schreiben → geschrieben
    trinken → getrunken   helfen → geholfen

Much the same is true of irregular English verbs such as:

    to write → wrote
    to drink → drunk

"Mixed" verbs are verbs which follow the pattern of regular (weak) verbs BUT have a vowel change. The past participle of these verbs ends in **-t**, as in:

    bringen → gebracht   denken → gedacht   wissen → gewusst

No **ge-** is added when the verb starts with a prefix which does not separate. These prefixes are: **be-, emp-, ent-, er-, ge-, miss-, ver-** and **zer-**
    Example: beginnen → begonnen   verlieren → verloren

lesen

ich habe .... gelesen	*I read, have read, have been reading*
du hast .... gelesen	*you read, have read, have been reading*
Sie haben .... gelesen	*you read, have read, have been reading*
er/sie/es/man hat gelesen	*he/she/it/one read, has read, has been reading*
Sam hat .... gelesen	*Sam read, has read, has been reading*
wir haben .... gelesen	*we read, have read, have been reading*
ihr habt .... gelesen	*you read, have read, have been reading*
Sie haben .... gelesen	*you read, have read, have been reading*
sie haben .... gelesen	*they read, have read, have been reading*
die Kinder haben gelesen	*the children read, have read, have been reading*

gehen*
	ich bin .... gegangen	*I went, have gone, have been going*
	du bist .... gegangen	*you went, have gone, have been going*
	Sie sind .... gegangen	*you went, have gone, have been going*
	er/sie/es/man ist . gegangen	*he/she/it/one went, has gone, has been going*
	Sam ist .... gegangen	*Sam went, has gone, has been going*
	wir sind .... gegangen	*we went, have gone, have been going*
	ihr seid .... gegangen	*you went, have gone, have been going*
	Sie sind .... gegangen	*you went, have gone, have been going*
	sie sind .... gegangen	*they went, have gone, have been going*
	die Kinder sind... gegangen	*the children went, have gone, have been going*

bringen
	ich habe .... gebracht	*I brought, have brought, used to bring*
	du hast .... gebracht	*you brought, have brought, used to bring*
	Sie haben............ gebracht	*you brought, have brought, used to bring*
	er/sie/es/man hat gebracht	*he/she/it/one brought, has brought, used to bring*
	Sam hat .... gebracht	*Sam brought, has brought, used to bring*
	wir haben .... gebracht	*we brought, have brought, used to bring*
	ihr habt .... gebracht	*you brought, have brought, used to bring*
	Sie haben............ gebracht	*you brought, have brought, used to bring*
	sie haben .... gebracht	*they brought, have brought, used to bring*
	die Kinder haben gebracht	*the children brought, have brought, used to bring*

(c) **haben or sein?**

The choice of **haben** or **sein** as auxiliary can cause some difficulty, as there is nothing quite like this distinction in English. Verbs of motion require **sein** as an auxiliary, and the following other **sein** verbs should be learnt:

aufwachen*, bleiben*, einschlafen*, geschehen*, passieren*, sein*, werden*

* indicates verbs which take **sein** as an auxiliary in Perfect tenses

IMPERFECT TENSE (also called Simple Past or Past) (**DAS PRÄTERITUM**)

The Imperfect is the past tense most commonly used in formal writing such as books and newspapers. Some common verbs are also used in the Imperfect in speech and informal writing. They are mixed freely with Perfect tenses. Like the Perfect, it translates a variety of English past tenses.

Therefore can mean:	Ich machte meine Hausaufgaben
	I did my homework
	I was doing my homework
	I used to do my homework
	I would do my homework (on Saturdays)

Some commonly used Imperfect verb forms include:

war, hatte, ging, machte, sah, kaufte, kam, spielte, es regnete, es schneite

German Grammar   *Verbs*

FORMATION OF THE IMPERFECT/SIMPLE PAST (DIE FORM DES PRÄTERITUMS)

(a) **Regular (weak) verbs**

Remove **-en** from the infinitive and add the following endings to the remaining stem:

	Singular			**Plural**	
1st person	ich	-te	wir	-ten
2nd person	du	-test	ihr	-tet
	Sie	-ten	Sie	-ten
3rd person	er/sie/es/man	-te	sie	-ten

Example:
- ich woh**nte**
- du wohn**test**
- Sie wohn**ten**
- er/sie/es/man wohn**te**
- Sam wohnte
- wir wohn**ten**
- ihr wohn**tet**
- Sie wohn**ten**
- sie wohn**ten**
- die Kinder wohn**ten**

(b) **Irregular (strong) verbs**

Because these verbs are irregular, the only safe way to discover the Imperfect stem is to look the verb up in a verb table. If the verb you are looking for does not seem to be in the table, it is possible that it is a compound of another verb, and therefore begins with one of the prefixes mentioned on pages 77 or 79.

Example: Compounds like **be**kommen and **an**kommen* *sep* behave in a similar way to **kommen***.

Some dictionaries and glossaries list only the vowel changes. So **sehen** would appear as **sehen (ie,a,e)**. The first vowel in the brackets is used in the 2nd and 3rd person singular Present. The second vowel is used in the Imperfect, and the final vowel is the past participle vowel.

The form you find in the irregular verb table (see page 84) is the 3rd (and 1st) person singular. To that, add the following endings:

	Singular			**Plural**	
1st person	ich	NONE	wir	-en
2nd person	du	-st	ihr	-t
	Sie	-en	Sie	-en
3rd person	er/sie/es/man	NONE	sie	-en

Example: **gehen*** - entry in verb table: **ging**
- ich..................ging
- du..................ging**st**
- Sie ....ging**en**
- er/sie/es/man ..ging
- wir..................ging**en**
- ihr..................ging**t**
- Sie ....ging**en**
- sie ....ging**en**

Tip: In practice, the Imperfect tense is much more common in the 3rd person singular and plural than in its other forms, because it is mainly used in books and newspapers. Nevertheless, you need to be sure of recognising it in the other persons, so be aware of them!

Verbs *German Grammar*

PLUPERFECT TENSE (DAS PLUSQUAMPERFEKT)

The Pluperfect is used in combination with either the Perfect or the Imperfect to denote actions in the past which happened before other actions in the past. This is similar to English usage.

Example:	ich **hatte** in Malvern **gewohnt**	ich **war** nach Hause **gegangen**
	I had lived in Malvern	*I had gone home*
Therefore can mean:	Ich hatte meine Hausaufgaben gemacht	
	I had done my homework	
	I had been doing my homework	

This tense uses the Imperfect tense of **haben** or **sein** as auxiliaries (Hilfsverben) and the past participle at the end of the main clause or sentence.

The choice of **haben** or **sein** as auxiliary is governed by the same rules as for the Perfect tense, page 54.

The past participle is formed in the same way as for the Perfect tense. So it has to be looked up for irregular (strong) and mixed verbs, but can be worked out for regular (weak) verbs.

The Pluperfect is often used after the conjunctions **nachdem** *after* and **sobald** *as soon as*:

Example: Nachdem ich gegessen hatte, ging es mir schlecht
After I had eaten, I was ill
Sobald ich meine Hausaufgaben gemacht hatte, bin ich in die Stadt gefahren
As soon as I had done my homework, I went into town

(a) **Regular (weak) verbs**

wohnen

ich hatte in Malvern gewohnt   wir hatten in Malvern gewohnt
du hattest in Malvern gewohnt   ihr hattet in Malvern gewohnt
Sie hatten in Malvern gewohnt   Sie hatten in Malvern gewohnt
er/sie/es/man hatte in York gewohnt   sie hatten in York gewohnt
Sam hatte in York gewohnt   die Kinder hatten in York gewohnt

(b) **Irregular (strong) verbs**

lesen

ich hatte ein Buch gelesen   wir hatten ein Buch gelesen
du hattest ein Buch gelesen   ihr hattet ein Buch gelesen
Sie hatten ein Buch gelesen   Sie hatten ein Buch gelesen
er/sie/es/man hatte ein Buch gelesen sie hatten ein Buch gelesen
Sam hatte ein Buch gelesen   die Kinder hatten ein Buch gelesen

gehen*
    ich war nach Hause gegangen   wir waren nach Hause gegangen
    du warst nach Hause gegangen   ihr wart nach Hause gegangen
    Sie waren nach Hause gegangen   Sie waren nach Hause gegangen
    er/sie/es/man war nach Hause gegangen   sie waren nach Hause gegangen
    Sam war nach Hause gegangen   die Omas waren nach Hause gegangen

verbringen
    ich hatte eine Woche verbracht   wir hatten eine Woche verbracht
    du hattest eine Woche verbracht   ihr hattet eine Woche verbracht
    Sie hatten eine Woche verbracht   Sie hatten eine Woche verbracht
    er/sie/es/man hatte eine Woche verbracht   sie hatten eine Woche verbracht
    Sam hatte eine Woche verbracht   die Omas hatten eine Woche verbracht

THE PASSIVE VOICE (DAS PASSIV)

For each tense, most verbs can be "active" or "passive" in voice. Verbs are "active" when the subject of the sentence (**ich, du, Sam, die Kinder**, etc) performs the action of the verb. For example, in the sentence: **Ich wasche das Auto**, the washing is done by **ich,** so it is an active sentence and has an active verb. This may be regarded as the "normal" form or voice.

In a sentence with a passive verb, the subject of the sentence suffers the action of the verb. So the previous example becomes: **Das Auto wird (von mir) gewaschen.** It would be quite possible to omit the **von mir**. This would leave the identity of the car washer open to speculation.

The passive is found rather more frequently in German than in English, and it is advisable to be able to recognise it when you see it.

There are two sorts of passive in German, the **werden**-passive and the **sein**-passive.

(a)   **The *werden*-passive**

This is the more common; it is used when a **process** is being carried out.

It is found in all the same tenses as the active verbs. Very often the Present passive is used in preference to the Future passive.

All verbs form their passive in the same way, regardless of whether they are irregular (strong) or regular (weak). The principle is that the appropriate tense of **werden** is used in conjunction with the past participle of the verb in question. The past participle is found at the end of the main clause or sentence as usual.

    Example: Die zwei Kinder **werden** von der Polizei **gesucht**
                          The two children are being sought by the police

Verbs   **German Grammar**

Present

ich werde ... gesucht	*I am (being) looked for*
du wirst ... gesucht	*you are (being) looked for*
Sie werden ... gesucht	*you are (being) looked for*
er/sie/es/man wird ... gesucht	*he/she/it/one is (being) looked for*
Sam wird ... gesucht	*Sam is (being) looked for*
wir werden ... gesucht	*we are (being) looked for*
ihr werdet ... gesucht	*you are (being) looked for*
Sie werden ... gesucht	*you are (being) looked for*
sie werden ... gesucht	*they are (being) looked for*
die Kinder werden ... gesucht	*the children are (being) looked for*
ich werde ... angerufen	*I am (being) phoned*
du wirst ... angerufen	*you are (being) phoned*
Sie werden ... angerufen	*you are (being) phoned*
er/sie/es/man wird ... angerufen	*he/she/it/one is (being) phoned*
Sam wird ... angerufen	*Sam is (being) phoned*
wir werden ... angerufen	*we are (being) phoned*
ihr werdet ... angerufen	*you are (being) phoned*
Sie werden ... angerufen	*you are (being) phoned*
sie werden ... angerufen	*they are (being) phoned*
die Kinder werden ... angerufen	*the children are (being) phoned*

Imperfect

ich wurde ... gesucht	*I was (being) looked for*
du wurdest ... gesucht	*you were (being) looked for*
Sie wurden ... gesucht	*you were (being) looked for*
er/sie/es/man wurde ... gesucht	*he/she/it/one was (being) looked for*
Sam wurde ... gesucht	*Sam was (being) looked for*
wir wurden ... gesucht	*we were (being) looked for*
ihr wurdet ... gesucht	*you were (being) looked for*
Sie wurden ... gesucht	*you were (being) looked for*
sie wurden ... gesucht	*they were (being) looked for*
die Kinder wurden ... gesucht	*the children were (being) looked for*
ich wurde ... angerufen	*I was (being) phoned*
du wurdest ... angerufen	*you were (being) phoned*
Sie wurden ... angerufen	*you were (being) phoned*
er/sie/es/man wurde ... angerufen	*he/she/it/one was (being) phoned*
Sam wurde ... angerufen	*Sam was (being) phoned*
wir wurden ... angerufen	*we were (being) phoned*
ihr wurdet ... angerufen	*you were (being) phoned*
Sie wurden ... angerufen	*you were (being) phoned*
sie wurden ... angerufen	*they were (being) phoned*
die Kinder wurden ... angerufen	*the children were (being) phoned*

Tip: There is NO UMLAUT on the auxiliary in this tense. Correct pronunciation is vital to avoid confusion.

Perfect

For the Perfect (and Pluperfect) passive a special form of the past participle of **werden** is used. **Worden** is used instead of **geworden** because a second **ge-** would sound clumsy.

ich bin ... gesucht worden	*I have been/was looked for*
du bist ... gesucht worden	*you have been/were looked for*
Sie sind ... gesucht worden	*you have been/were looked for*
er/sie/es/man ist ... gesucht worden	*he/she/it/one has been/was looked for*
Sam ist ... gesucht worden	*Sam is being/was looked for*
wir sind ... gesucht worden	*we have been/were looked for*
ihr seid .. gesucht worden	*you have been/were looked for*
Sie sind ... gesucht worden	*you have been/were looked for*
sie sind ... gesucht worden	*they have been/were looked for*
die Kinder sind ... gesucht worden	*the children have been/were looked for*

ich bin ... angerufen worden	*I have been/was phoned*
du bist ... angerufen worden	*you have been/were phoned*
Sie sind ... angerufen worden	*you have been/were phoned*
er/sie/es/man ist .. angerufen worden	*he/she/it/one has been/was phoned*
Sam ist ... angerufen worden	*Sam has been/was phoned*
wir sind ... angerufen worden	*we have been/were phoned*
ihr seid ... angerufen worden	*you have been/were phoned*
Sie sind ... angerufen worden	*you have been/were phoned*
sie sind ... angerufen worden	*they have been/were phoned*
die Kinder .. sind angerufen worden	*the children have been/were phoned*

(b) **The *sein*-passive**

The **sein**-passive is used to show the **state** the subject of the verb is in as a result of some action which took place earlier. The past participle could be looked upon as an adjective.

For both regular (weak) and irregular (strong) verbs it is formed by using the appropriate tense of **sein** and the past participle of the verb in question. It is most commonly found in the Present and Imperfect tenses.

Present tense

Ich bin verletzt	*I am injured*
Sam ist verletzt	*Sam is injured*

Imperfect tense

Ich war verletzt	*I was injured*
Sam war verletzt	*Sam was injured*

Tip: To decide whether to use the **werden**-passive or the **sein**-passive you have to be clear whether an **action** (therefore **werden**-passive) or a **state** (therefore **sein**-passive) is being described. The following pairs of examples will help:

Die Hausaufgaben **werden** gemacht   (action)
The homework is being done   (someone is even now doing the homework)
Die Hausaufgaben **sind** gemacht   (state)
The homework is done   (because someone has already done it)

Das alte Rathaus **wurde** 2000 abgerissen   (action)
The old Town Hall was pulled down in 2000 (the action took place that year)
Das alte Rathaus **war** (schon) 2000 abgerissen   (state)
The old Town Hall was (already) pulled down in 2000
                                          (the action had taken place at some time beforehand)

If you really cannot decide between the two sorts of passive, remember that the **werden**-passive is about four times as common as the **sein**-passive.

THE AGENT IN THE PASSIVE

The passive is often used without stating clearly who performed the action. It is possible, however, to say who or what performed the action, translating the English *by*.

There are three possibilities:

(i)   **von** + Dative - 'agent, either human or inanimate'

       Der Junge wurde **von dem Mädchen** gesehen
       *The boy was seen **by the girl***
       Das Auto wurde **vom Gewitter** gewaschen
       *The car was washed **by the thunderstorm***

(ii)   **mit** + Dative - 'instrument'

       Der Mann wurde **mit einem Messer** erstochen
       *The man was (fatally) stabbed **with a knife***

       If *by* or *with* can be replaced by *with the help of* then you need to use **mit**.

(iii) **durch** + Accusative - 'means'

       Er wurde **durch kaltes Wasser** geweckt
       *He was woken **by means of cold water***

German Grammar — Verbs

ALTERNATIVES TO THE PASSIVE (ALTERNATIVEN ZUM PASSIV)

There are various ways of expressing the same or similar meanings to the passive.

(i) Using **man**

This is often used if there is no clue as to the identity of the subject.

> Letzte Woche hat **man** mein Fahrrad gestohlen
> *Person or persons unknown stole my bike last week*
> *They stole my bike last week*
> *Someone stole my bike last week*

(ii) Using a reflexive

> Die Haustür öffnete **sich**
> *The front door opened (itself)*

Verbs   ***German Grammar***

CONDITIONS (BEDINGUNGSSÄTZE)

Conditional sentences show actions which would happen, usually if some other condition is met, as in English. There are various sorts of conditional sentence in German. Each sort has a **wenn**-clause and a consequence clause.

(a)   **Open conditions**

The open condition is really **a statement of fact**.
The **wenn**-clause has the Present tense, the consequence clause has the Future or Present tense.

     Example:

            Ich **werde** mit Sabine Tennis **spielen, wenn** sie Zeit **hat**
            I shall play tennis with Sabine if she has time
            Wenn es um acht Uhr **regnet, fahre** ich mit dem Bus zur Schule
            If it is raining at eight o'clock I go to school by bus

(b)   **Possibilities**

The second sort of condition concerns things which **might** - or **might not** - happen. It is sometimes called the "unreal" or "impossible" condition.

The **wenn**-clause often uses Konjunktiv II, and the consequence clause often uses a conditional formed by **würde** plus the infinitive.

At this level, it is probably best to learn the sentence patterns.

     Example:

            Ich **würde** dich gern **besuchen, wenn** ich genug Geld **hätte**
            I would like to visit you if I had enough money

            Wir **würden** glücklich **sein, wenn** es zu Mittag Pizza **gäbe**
            We would be pleased if there was pizza for lunch

            Wenn das Wetter besser **wäre, könnten** wir spazieren **gehen**
            If the weather was better we could go for a walk

            Die Schüler **wären** glücklich, **wenn** die Schuluniform modernisiert **würde**
            The children would be delighted if the school uniform was brought up to date

Tip: It doesn't matter whether the **wenn**-clause or the consequence clause comes first in a sentence, although, of course, the word order rules must be obeyed.

(c) Modal verbs (Modalverben)

The modal verbs can be used in their conditional form.

>Example:
>>Ich **könnte** eine ganze Torte **essen,** wenn ich richtig Appetit **hätte**
>>*I could eat a whole cake if I was really hungry*

See also MODAL VERBS, pages 65-69.

THE SUBJUNCTIVE (DER KONJUNKTIV)

Most uses of the subjunctive (*Konjunktiv*) are beyond the scope of this grammar guide. However, some of them will be worth knowing at this level.

(a) Softening the tone of a Request

To moderate the tone of a statement or request, *Konjunktiv II* is often used, especially colloquially. For strong verbs the *Konjunktiv II* is formed by adding an *Umlaut* to the Imperfect tense vowel if this is possible.

>Example:
>>Ich **hätte** gern eine Tasse Kaffee
>>*I would like a cup of coffee*
>>So, das **wär**'s
>>*So, that's all*
>>**Könnten** Sie mir bitte **sagen,** wie ich am besten zur Post komme?
>>*Could you please tell the best way to get to the post office?*

(b) Wishes

Some set phrases use what is in fact *Konjunktiv I* for (often pious) wishes. It is best to learn them as vocabulary at this stage.

>Example:
>>Gott **sei** Dank!
>>*Thank God!*
>>Es **lebe** die Republik!
>>*Long live the Republic!*

Verbs   *German Grammar*

COMMAND FORMS/IMPERATIVES (DER IMPERATIV)

There are four command forms (imperatives) for every verb. These are based on the Present tense.

In order to decide which form to use, you need to know who you are talking to.

(a)   **For people you would normally call *du***

Remove the **-st** from the **du**-form of the Present tense. Add an exclamation mark! This is the same for both regular (weak) and irregular (strong) verbs. However, if there is an Umlaut on the vowel of an irregular (strong) verb, remove it.

       Example: du spielst →   Spiel!
                       du kommst →   Komm!
                       du isst etwas →   Iss etwas!
                       du fährst langsamer →   Fahr langsamer!

Sometimes an **-e** is added after a **d, h** or **t**

       Example: du findest dein Portemonnaie → Finde dein Portmonnaie!
                       du suchst dein Portemonnaie → Suche dein Portemonnaie!
                       du wartest auf den Bus → Warte auf den Bus!

(b)   **For people you would normally call *ihr***

Use the **ihr** form of the Present tense, but without the **ihr**. This is the same for both regular (weak) and irregular (strong) verbs. Add an exclamation mark!

       Example: ihr spielt →   Spielt!
                       ihr kommt →   Kommt!
                       ihr fahrt langsamer → Fahrt langsamer!
                       ihr esst etwas →   Esst etwas!

(c)   **For people you would normally call *Sie***

Use the **Sie** form of the Present tense with the **Sie** coming after the verb. This is the same for both regular (weak) and irregular (strong) verbs. Add an exclamation mark!

       Example: Sie spielen →   Spielen Sie!
                       Sie kommen →   Kommen Sie!
                       Sie fahren langsamer → Fahren Sie langsamer!
                       Sie essen etwas →   Essen Sie etwas!

(d)   **Translating *Let's***

Use the **wir** form of the Present tense with the **wir** coming after the verb. This is the same for both regular (weak) and irregular (strong) verbs. Add an exclamation mark!

Example:	Wir spielen →	Spielen wir!	*Let's play!*
	Wir gehen→	Gehen wir!	*Let's go!*
	Wir fahren langsam →	Fahren wir langsam!	*Let's drive slowly*
	Wir essen etwas →	Essen wir etwas!	*Let's eat something*

It is also possible to use **lassen** + **uns**. Again, this applies to both irregular (strong) and regular (weak) verbs.

Example:	Lass uns zu Fuß nach Hause gehen
	Let's walk home

(e) The verb 'sein'

The verb **sein** *to be* is irregular. You should learn these forms.

	Du bist still→	Sei still!	*Be quiet!*
	Wir sind still→	Seien wir still!	*Let's be quiet!*
	Ihr seid still→	Seid still!	*Be quiet!*
	Sie sind still→	Seien Sie still!	*Be quiet!*

MODAL VERBS (MODALVERBEN)

In German there is a group of verbs which are used with the infinitive of another verb (the dependent infinitive). These are the modal verbs. Anyone who learnt: **Ich kann Hockey spielen,** etc in the first weeks of learning German will know them. They can express a whole variety of subtle meanings.

The modal verbs are:
        dürfen   können   mögen   müssen   sollen   wollen

When it means "to have something done" (as opposed to doing it yourself) the verb **lassen** can behave in much the same way as a modal verb. (See page 86)

(a) Formation of Present Tense

dürfen	**können**	**mögen**	**müssen**	**sollen**	**wollen**
ich darf	ich kann	ich mag	ich muss	ich soll	ich will
du darfst	du kannst	du magst	du musst	du sollst	du willst
er darf	er kann	er mag	er muss	er soll	er will
sie darf	sie kann	sie mag	sie muss	sie soll	sie will
man darf	man kann	man mag	man muss	man soll	man will
Sam darf	Sam kann	Sam mag	Sam muss	Sam soll	Sam will
wir dürfen	wir können	wir mögen	wir müssen	wir sollen	wir wollen
ihr dürft	ihr könnt	ihr mögt	ihr müsst	ihr sollt	ihr wollt
Sie dürfen	Sie können	Sie mögen	Sie müssen	Sie sollen	Sie wollen
sie dürfen	sie können	sie mögen	sie müssen	sie sollen	sie wollen

(b) Word Order With Modal Verbs

In a simple sentence, the modal verb occupies the "verb" word order position. The dependent infinitive comes at the end of the main clause.

Example: Ich **will** heute Abend **fernsehen**, aber ich **muss** zuerst **spülen**.
I want to watch TV this evening but I have to wash up first

In subordinate clauses the same principle applies. The modal verb comes at the end of the subordinate clause, after the dependent infinitive.

Example: Ich habe den Film nicht gesehen, weil ich nicht **ausgehen durfte**
I didn't see the film because I wasn't allowed out

(c) Tenses other than the Present

In tenses other than the Present, only the tense of the modal verb changes. The dependent infinitive remains the same.

Example: Sie **wollte** ihn aber nicht **anrufen**
But she didn't want to phone him
Sie **wird** kommen **müssen**
She will have to come

Note that the commonly used conditional forms are:

mögen →	ich/er möchte	*I/he would like*
können →	ich/er könnte	*I/he could, I/he might*
sollen →	ich/er sollte	*I/he ought to, I/he should*

(d) Missing out the Dependent Infinitive

The dependent infinitive can sometimes be left out after modal verbs if it is clear from the context what it should be. Usually, this is a verb of motion or the verb **tun**.

Example: Sam **will** nach Berlin
Sam wants to go to Berlin
Sie **könnten** morgen vielleicht ins Schwimmbad
They/You could go to the swimming pool tomorrow
Das **darfst** du nicht
You are not allowed to do that

The following common idiomatic phrases work on the same principle:

Example: Ich **kann** nicht mehr
I can't go on
Was **soll** das?
What's the meaning of this?

Meanings of Modal Verbs

Modal verbs have very subtle meanings. A further complication is the fact that their meaning sometimes changes after **nicht**. Examples are given for each modal verb to provide guidance.

dürfen

(a) It usually means "to be allowed to".

Example: Ich **darf** den Film sehen
I am allowed to see the film, I may see the film

(b) It means "must not" after **nicht**. See also **müssen**.

Example: In der U-Bahn **darf** man **nicht** rauchen
You must not smoke in the Underground

Tip: Note the idiom:
Das **darf nicht** wahr sein
That can't be true

(c) When politeness is intended it is frequently used as a substitute for **können**:

Example: Was **darf** es sein?
What would you like?
Darf ich bitten?
Would you like to dance?

können

(a) It usually means "to be able to".

Example: Ich **kann** Tennis spielen
I can/am able to play tennis
Der Kanzler **konnte** leider nicht kommen
Unfortunately the Chancellor wasn't able to come

Tip: Notice that the Imperfect tense is konnte **without** an Umlaut

(b) Like the English "may, could, might", it can express possibility.

Example: Das **kann** wohl sein
That may well be so
Sie **könnte** vielleicht um acht Uhr anrufen
She might perhaps phone at eight o'clock

Verbs   *German Grammar*

(c) It can be used with the meaning "to know how to do something".

    Example: Sie **kann** gut Deutsch
                        She can speak German well
                        Ich **kann** Klavier spielen
                        I know how to play the piano

(d) Colloquially, it is often used instead of **dürfen**.

    Example: **Kannst** du den Film sehen?
                        Are you allowed to see the film?

mögen

It means "to like".

    Example: Ich **mag** Kassetten hören
                        I like listening to cassettes
                        Sie **möchte** eine Tasse Tee
                        She would like a cup of tea
                        Sam **mochte** seinen Bruder nicht
                        Sam did not like his brother

müssen

(a) It usually means "to have to".

    Example: Sam **muss** jetzt gehen
                        Sam has to go now
                        Das **musste** man einfach probieren
                        You just had to try it!
                        Muss das sein?
                        Is that really necessary?

(b) With **nicht** it means "needn't" or "don't have to".

    Example: Wir **müssen** die Aufgabe nicht für morgen machen
                        We don't have to/needn't do the homework for tomorrow

Tip: "mustn't" is usually translated by *darf nicht*. (See dürfen (b), page 67)
But *Ich brauche nicht* is usually preferred to the negative of *müssen*

    Example: Du brauchst heute nicht zur Schule zu gehen
                        You don't have to go to school today

(c) It can express logical deduction.

    Example: zweimal X gleicht Y, also **muss** viermal X zweimal Y gleichen
                        $2X = Y$, *so $4X$ must equal $2Y$*

sollen

(a) It usually means "to have to, to be obliged to".
Often, there is an external obligation

Example: Um wie viel Uhr **sollte** der Zug ankommen?
When should the train arrive?
Du **solltest** deiner Großmutter eine Geburtstagskarte schicken
You ought to send your grandmother a birthday card

(b) It can often be the equivalent of a command.

Example: Sam **soll** am Rathaus auf mich warten
Sam is to wait for me at the Town Hall
Du **sollst** nicht stehlen
Thou shalt not steal

(c) It can be used to express an intention, with the meaning "are to", "is supposed to".

Example: Hier **soll** der neue Sprachblock sein
This is where the new Languages Block is to be
Was **soll** das heißen?
What's that supposed to mean?
Wann und wo **sollen** wir uns sehen?
When and where shall we see each other?

wollen

(a) It usually means "to want to", "to wish to".

Example: Ich **will** dir helfen
I want to help you
Sam **wollte** früher abfahren
Sam wanted to leave earlier
Essen Sie so viel Sie **wollen!**
Eat as much as you like

(b) It can be used to express willingness or consent.

Example: **Willst** du mit mir in die Disco gehen?
Will you come to the disco with me?
Er **will** den Hund nicht verkaufen
He won't sell the dog

(c) It can be used to express intention.

Example: Wir **wollen** nächstes Jahr nach Japan fahren
We're hoping to go to Japan next year
Er **wollte** gerade ausgehen, als du angekommen bist
He was just about to go out when you arrived

THE INFINITIVE (DER INFINITIV)

FORMS OF THE INFINITIVE (INFINITIVFORMEN)

(a) The infinitive is the part of the verb listed in a dictionary, and means "to ...". In German the infinitive nearly always ends in -**en**.

>   Example: spielen   *to play*
>   trinken   *to drink*
>   sein*   *to be*

(b) Many verbs also have a passive infinitive, which is the past participle of the verb with **werden** or **sein**. (see PASSIVE, pages 57-61)

>   Example: gekauft werden   *to be bought*
>   getrunken werden *to be drunk*
>   vergessen sein   *to be forgotten*

THE INFINITIVE WITH ZU (DER INFINITIV MIT ZU)

The infinitive with **zu** is found at the end of its clause.

> Example: Ich beabsichtige, im kommenden Sommer nach Österreich **zu fahren**
> *I intend to travel to Austria next summer*

For separable verbs the **zu** is inserted between the separable prefix and the verb and written as a single word.

> Example: Ich habe vor, heute Abend **auszugehen**
> *I intend to go out this evening*

The infinitive with **zu** is used:

(a) after certain prepositions

    (i)   **um ... zu** *in order to, to*

> Example: Anne geht ins Wohnzimmer, **um** ein Mathematikbuch **zu lesen**
> *Anne is going into the lounge to read a Maths book*

    (ii)   **ohne ... zu** *without*

> Example: Er kaufte das Auto, **ohne** an die Kosten **zu denken**
> *He bought the car without thinking of the costs*

(iii) **statt ... zu/anstatt ... zu** *instead of*

Example: Er hat ferngesehen, **anstatt** seinem Vater **zu helfen**
He watched TV instead of helping his father

(iv) **außer ... zu** *except /besides*

Example: Was konnten wir, **außer zu hoffen**?
What else could we do except hope?

(b) after the following verbs:

(i) bekommen *to get*

Example: Wenn ich den Dieb **zu fassen bekomme** ...
If I get my hands on the thief ...

(ii) bleiben* *to remain*

Example: Diese Briefe **bleiben** noch **zu schreiben**
These letters remain to be written

(iii) brauchen *to need*

Example: Du **brauchst** nicht **zu kommen**
You don't need to come

(iv) scheinen *to seem*

Example: Der Torwart **schien** den Ball nicht **zu sehen**
The goalkeeper didn't seem to see the ball

(v) versprechen *to promise*

Example: Monika **verspricht** heute Pizza **zu backen**
Monika promises to make pizza today

(vi) wissen *to know how to*

Example: Sie weiß mit allerlei Problemen fertig **zu werden**
She knows how to deal with all sorts of problems

(c) after the adjectives **einfach, interessant, leicht, schwer, schwierig**

Example: Dieses Buch ist **interessant zu lesen**
This book is interesting to read

(d) in comparative phrases

> Example: Man sollte **lieber** ein Hobby aufnehmen, **als** nur **fernzusehen**
> *It is better to take up a hobby than just to watch TV*

(e) in exclamations

> Example: Ach, in Tahiti **zu sein**!
> *Oh, to be in Tahiti!*

(f) in small ads in the newspaper

> Example: Ferienwohnung **zu vermieten**
> *Holiday home to let*

THE INFINITIVE WITHOUT ZU (DER INFINITIV OHNE ZU)

The infinitive without **zu** is found at the end of the main clause. See also WORD ORDER

(a) with the modal verbs **dürfen, können, mögen, müssen, sollen** and **wollen**

> Example: Er **will** eine Hose **kaufen**
> *He wants to buy a pair of trousers*

Much fuller details are given under MODAL VERBS, pages 65-69.

(b) after some verbs of perception: **fühlen, hören, sehen, spüren**

> Example: Ich **sah** sie **ankommen**
> *I saw her arrive*

(c) after **lassen**, meaning to have someone do something for you

> Example: Ich **lasse** meinen Wagen immer **reparieren**. Ich kann das selber nicht
> *I always have my car repaired. I can't do it myself*

(d) after certain verbs of motion – **fahren*, gehen*, kommen*, schicken**
The verb in the infinitive gives the reason for going.

> Example: Maria **geht** jetzt **schlafen**
> *Maria is going to bed*
> Vati **fährt** in zehn Minuten **einkaufen**
> *Dad is going shopping in ten minutes' time*

(e) after **bleiben*, finden** and **haben** followed by a verb of place

> Example: Der Bus **blieb** plötzlich **stehen**
> *The bus suddenly halted*
> Sie **fand** die Kinder wieder vor dem Computer **sitzen**
> *She found the children sitting in front of the computer again*

(f) in some idioms

> Example: Das **nennst** du **spülen!**
> *Do you call that washing-up?*
> Sie **lehrte** mich **Eis laufen**
> *She taught me how to skate*
> Opa **legt** sich oft im Wohnzimmer **schlafen**
> *Grandpa often lies down for a sleep in the living room*

THE INFINITIVE USED AS A NOUN (DER INFINITIV ALS SUBSTANTIV)

(a) The infinitive of most German verbs can be used as a noun. They are all neuter, do not normally appear in the plural, and all have a capital letter. When using a reflexive verb as a noun the **sich** is omitted.

> Example: Das unendliche **Herumfahren** nervte den Taxifahrer
> *The endless **driving around** got on the taxi driver's nerves*

(b) Infinitive nouns are often compounded with another element to make a longer word.

> Example: Zu schnelles **Autofahren** sieht die Polizei nicht so gern
> *The Police do not approve of speeding*

(c) Infinitive nouns are used with prepositions. These are best learnt as idioms.

    (i) **beim** + infinitive: **Beim Fußballspielen** hat er sich den Fuß verrenkt
                                          While playing football he twisted his ankle
    (ii) **ins** + infinitive: Das Motorrad geriet **ins Schleudern**
                                            The motorbike went into a skid

PARTICIPLES (PARTIZIPIEN)

There are two participles in German, the past participle (see the Perfect tense, pages 52-54) and the Present participle.

PAST PARTICIPLE (DAS PARTIZIP PERFEKT)

For regular (weak) verbs the past participle is usually formed by adding the prefix **ge-** to the infinitive, removing the **-en** and replacing it with **-t**.

For irregular (strong) verbs the past participle usually begins with **ge-** and ends in **-en**. You may need to refer to the irregular verb table (page 84) for vowel changes.

(a) As well as being used as a part of a verb, it can be used as an adjective, taking an adjective ending like any other adjective.

> Example: die **geöffnete** Weinflasche   *the open(ed) wine bottle*
>   mein **geschwollener** Fuß   *my swollen foot*

(b) A few idioms use past participle constructions

> MWSt und Bedienung **inbegriffen** *VAT and service inclusive*
> **Verdammt!** *Damn!*
> wie **gesagt** *as I said*
> wie **erwartet** *as expected*

PRESENT PARTICIPLE (PRÄSENS PARTIZIP)

This is formed for both regular (weak) and irregular (strong) verbs by adding **-d** to the infinitive.

> Example: lachen → lachend   *laughing*

Tip: NEVER use the Present participle as part of an attempt to translate the English continuous forms such as "I was laughing". Use the Imperfect **Ich lachte**.

(a) As well as being used as a part of a verb, it can be used as an adjective, taking an adjective ending like any other adjective.

> Example: im **kommenden** Sommer   *in the coming summer*

(b) Like other adjectives, they may be used as adverbs.

> Example: Er lernte **überraschend** schnell Englisch
> *He learnt English surprisingly quickly*

(c) Like other adjectives, they may be used as nouns. They take endings. See page 8.

> Example: der/die **Auszubildende**   *the apprentice/trainee*

VERBS FOLLOWED BY THE NOMINATIVE (VERBEN MIT NOMINATIV)

These verbs are followed by the Nominative case:

> sein*   *to be*
> heißen   *to be called*
> werden*   *to become*
> bleiben* *to remain*

> Example: Das ist **mein neuer Computer**
> *That is my new computer*
> Er heißt **Herr Grün**
> *He is called Herr Grün*
> Fritz wurde **ein glücklicher Vater**
> *Fritz became a happy father*
> Du bleibst **mein bester Freund**
> *You remain my best friend*

Verbs Followed by the Dative (Verben mit Dativ)

These verbs are used with the Dative case. This seems a bit strange to English-speaking learners of German. Sadly, the only known cure is to learn which they are!

(a) Common verbs which take the Dative include:

    danken   *to thank*
    folgen*   *to follow*
    helfen   *to help*

Example: Ich muss **dir** für das nette Geschenk danken
I must thank you for the lovely present
Sherlock Holmes ist **dem Dieb** gefolgt
Sherlock Holmes followed the thief
Ich habe **meinem Vater** in der Küche geholfen
I helped my father in the kitchen

(b) Less common ones include:

    antworten   *to answer*
    begegnen*   *to meet (by chance/for the first time)*
    gehören   *to belong to*
    passen   *to suit*
    wehtun (sep)   *to hurt*
    zuhören (sep)   *to listen to*

Example: Sie hat **der Musik** gut zugehört
She listened carefully to the music
Meine Hand tut **mir** weh
My hand hurts

(c) Verbs such as **passieren*** and **geschehen*** meaning to "happen to someone" are used with a Dative:

Example: So etwas ist **deinem Vater** nie passiert
Nothing like that ever happened to your father

Impersonal Verbs (Unpersönliche Verben)

Some verbs are used with the subject **es**. These are known as impersonal verbs, because the identity of **es** is vague. They include the following:

(a) Weather verbs

Example: Es regnet   *It is raining*
Es friert   *It is freezing*

Verbs   *German Grammar*

(b)   Verbs referring to noises and other natural occurrences

           Example: Es klingelte
                          The doorbell rang
                      Hier zieht es
                      It's draughty here
                      Besuch ist wie Fisch. Nach drei Tagen stinkt es
                      Visitors are like fish. After three days they stink

(c)   With **sein** and **werden**

           Example: Es ist spät   *It is late*
                      Es wurde kalt   *It got cold*
                      Es ist mir kalt   *I am cold*

(d)   In various idioms

                     Wie geht es dir?   *How are you?*
                     Es kommt darauf an   *It depends*
                     Es macht nichts   *It doesn't matter*
                     Es gefällt mir   *I like it*
                     Es gelingt mir   *I succeed*
                     Es tut mir Leid   *I am sorry*
                     Es reicht mir   *That's enough for me*
                     Es schmeckt mir nicht   *I don't like the taste*

REFLEXIVE VERBS (REFLEXIVE VERBEN)

In German there are three sorts of reflexive verb:

(a)   Those verbs which have an Accusative reflexive pronoun. The reflexive pronoun must not be omitted.

These include:

                    sich beeilen   *to hurry*
                    sich erkälten   *to catch a cold*
                    sich verabschieden   *to say goodbye*

For reference, the Present tense of **sich erkälten** is given below:

                   ich erkälte mich   *I catch cold, I am catching cold*
                   du erkältest dich   *you catch cold, you are catching cold*
                   Sie erkälten sich   *you catch cold, you are catching cold*
                   er/sie/es/man erkältet sich   *he/she/it/one catches, is catching cold*
                   Sam erkältet sich   *Sam catches cold, is catching cold*
                   wir erkälten uns   *we catch cold, we are catching cold*
                   ihr erkältet euch   *you catch cold, you are catching cold*
                   Sie erkälten sich   *you catch cold, you are catching cold*
                   sie erkälten sich   *they catch cold, they are catching cold*
                   die Kinder erkälten sich   *the children catch cold, are catching cold*

Verbs

(b) Those verbs which are being used reflexively: (See page 38)

    Example: sich fragen   *to wonder*
                 sich rasieren   *to shave (oneself)*
                 sich waschen   *to wash (oneself)*

(c) Those verbs which have a Dative reflexive pronoun in addition to an Accusative object. For reference, an example is written out below:

    ich habe mir die Hände gewaschen
    du hast dir die Hände gewaschen
    Sie haben sich die Hände gewaschen
    er/sie/es/man hat sich die Hände gewaschen
    Sam hat sich die Hände gewaschen
    wir haben uns die Hände gewaschen
    ihr habt euch die Hände gewaschen
    Sie haben sich die Hände gewaschen
    sie haben sich die Hände gewaschen
    die Kinder haben sich die Hände gewaschen

Tip: Sometimes these expressions are given as **sich die Hände waschen** in vocabularies. The **sich** is Dative, not Accusative. Beware!

SEPARABLE VERBS (TRENNBARE VERBEN)

(a) Common separable prefixes are:
ab-, an-, auf-, aus-, ein-, fern-, fort-, her-, hin-, mit-, nach-, vor-, vorbei-, weg-, weiter-, zu-, zurück-, zusammen-

(b) If the separable verb is the only verb in a main clause, the prefix is the last word in the sentence. This is also true for command forms.

    Example: Er sieht gern **fern**
                 He likes watching TV
                 Rufen Sie mich morgen **an**!
                 Phone me tomorrow

If the separable verb is the second verb in the main clause, the verb remains together and is the last word in the sentence.

    Example: Er will uns **ab**holen
                 He wants to pick us up
                 Ich werde morgen Abend **an**kommen
                 I shall arrive tomorrow evening

(c) In a subordinate clause the verb is the last word and does **not** separate.

    Example: Als er das Fenster **zu**machte, ...
                 When he closed the window, ...
                 Wenn ich zu Hause **an**komme, ...
                 When I arrive home, ...

Verbs German Grammar

(d) The past participle of a separable verb is formed by slipping the **ge** between the prefix and the main part of the verb, following the rules for forming the past participle, see pages 52-54.

Example: aufmachen → auf**ge**macht *opened*
aussteigen* → aus**ge**stiegen *got off (train, etc)*

(e) In the same way, if the separable verb is the second verb in the sentence and **zu** is needed, **zu** slips between the two parts of the verb.

Example: Er hoffte, heute Abend aus**zu**gehen
He hoped to go out tonight

(f) Separable verbs have a prefix which can separate from the main part of the verb. For changes in irregular (strong) verbs you may have to check the verb without its prefix in a dictionary or the irregular verb table, page 84.

Example: einsteigen* *to get on (bus, etc)*
Look up: steigen* *to climb*

(g) Common regular (weak) separable verbs are:

abholen	*to fetch*	einkaufen	*to shop*
ablehnen	*to refuse*	einpacken	*to pack*
abräumen	*to clear away*	fortsetzen	*to continue*
anmachen	*to switch on*	hinzufügen	*to add*
aufhören	*to stop*	sich hinsetzen	*to sit down*
aufmachen	*to open*	vorbereiten	*to prepare*
aufpassen	*to pay attention*	sich vorstellen	*to introduce*
aufräumen	*to tidy up*	zuhören	*to listen to*
aufwachen*	*to wake up*	zumachen	*to close*
ausmachen	*to switch off*	zurückkehren*	*to return*
auspacken	*to unpack*		

(h) Common irregular (strong) separable verbs are:

abfahren*	*to depart*	einladen	*to invite*
anfangen	*to begin*	einschlafen*	*to fall asleep*
ankommen*	*to arrive*	einsteigen*	*to get on*
anrufen	*to telephone*	hineingehen*	*to go in*
anziehen	*to put on (clothes)*	mitnehmen	*to take with*
sich anziehen	*to get dressed*	stattfinden	*to take place*
aufstehen*	*to get up*	umsteigen*	*to change (train)*
ausgeben	*to spend (money)*	sich umziehen	*to get changed*
ausgehen*	*to go out*	vorhaben	*to intend*
aussteigen*	*to get out*	vorlesen	*to read aloud*
ausziehen	*to take off (clothes)*	vorschlagen	*to suggest*
sich ausziehen	*to get undressed*	vorziehen	*to prefer*

* takes **sein** in the Perfect tense

(i) Separable verbs are usually shown in the dictionary by the abbreviation *sep* after the infinitive.

INSEPARABLE VERBS (UNTRENNBARE VERBEN)

(a) The following prefixes do not separate from the verb:

be-, emp-, ent-, er-, ge-, miss-, ver- and **zer-**

These verbs have no **ge** prefix in the past participle.

Example: Ich habe meine Oma **besucht**
I visited my grandmother

(b) Common regular (weak) inseparable verbs are:

übersetzen	*to translate*	überraschen	*to surprise*
überreden	*to persuade*	untersuchen	*to investigate*
wiederholen	*to repeat*		

Example: Ich habe ihn **überredet** mitzukommen
I persuaded him to come with me

(c) Common irregular (strong) inseparable verbs are:

überfahren	*to run over*	sich übergeben	*to be sick*
übertreiben	*to exaggerate*	umgeben	*to surround*
sich unterhalten	*to talk*	unterbrechen	*to interrupt*
unterscheiden	*to distinguish*		

Example: Ich **unterhalte mich** mit meinen Freunden
I talk to my friends
Der Kleine **hat sich übergeben**
The little one has been sick

SEPARABLE OR INSEPARABLE VERBS (TRENNBARE ODER UNTRENNBARE VERBEN)

The prefixes **durch-, hinter-, über-, um-, unter-, wider-** and **wieder-** can be either separable or inseparable. When you meet one of these verbs, you must learn whether it is separable or inseparable. If it is inseparable, the prefix stays with its verb at all times and the past participle is formed without **ge**.

Example: Er hat die Katze **überfahren** (inseparable)
He ran over the cat

Verbs Followed by a Preposition (Verben mit Präpositionen)

Many verbs are idiomatically followed by a particular preposition. Here, the prepositions are listed alphabetically.

(a) an + Dative

teilnehmen an *sep*	*to take part in*
Es fehlt mir an	*I lack*

(b) an + Accusative

sich erinnern an	*to remember*
sich gewöhnen an	*to get used to*

(c) auf + Accusative

sich freuen auf	*to look forward to*
sich konzentrieren auf	*to concentrate on*
warten auf	*to wait for*

(d) aus + Dative

bestehen aus	*to consist of*

(e) für + Accusative

danken für	*to thank for*
halten für	*to consider*
sich interessieren für	*to be interested in*

(f) mit + Dative

aufhören mit *sep*	*to stop doing something*
telefonieren mit	*to speak on the phone with*
sich unterhalten mit	*to converse with*
vergleichen mit	*to compare with*
zusammenstoßen* mit *sep*	*to collide with*

(g) nach + Dative

sich erkundigen nach	*to enquire after*
fragen nach	*to ask after*
rufen nach	*to call after, to call for*
schmecken nach	*to taste of (usually something bad)*
suchen nach	*to search for*
telefonieren nach	*to phone for (a doctor)*

(h) über + Accusative

sich ärgern über	*to be annoyed about*
sich freuen über	*to be pleased about*
sich informieren über	*to find out about*
schreiben über	*to write about*
sprechen über	*to discuss*
sich streiten über	*to argue over*
sich wundern über	*to be surprised at*

(i) um + Accusative

sich handeln um	*to be a question of, to be a matter of*
ums Leben kommen*	*to die*

(j) von + Dative

abhängen von *sep*	*to depend on*
sich erholen von	*to recover from*
erzählen von	*to tell of, to tell about*
hören von	*to hear of*
lesen von	*to read about*
träumen von	*to dream of*

(k) vor + Dative

Angst haben vor	*to be frightened of*
retten vor	*to save from*
warnen vor	*to warn about*

(l) zu + Dative

einladen zu *sep*	*to invite to*
veranlassen zu	*to cause to*

Verbs   *German Grammar*

REGULAR (WEAK) VERBS (REGELMÄßIGE (SCHWACHE) VERBEN)

The verbs below follow the same pattern as *spielen*.

Infinitive	Present	Imperfect	Perfect	Meaning
spielen	ich spiele	ich spielte	ich habe gespielt	*to play*

Infinitive	Meaning	Infinitive	Meaning
abholen *sep*	*to pick up, fetch*	hören	*to hear*
abräumen *sep*	*to clear away*	kapieren†	*to understand*
anmachen *sep*	*to switch on*	kaufen	*to buy*
antworten†	*to answer*	klingeln	*to ring*
arbeiten†	*to work*	klopfen	*to knock*
aufhören *sep*	*to stop*	kriegen	*to get*
aufmachen *sep*	*to open*	lachen	*to laugh*
aufpassen *sep*	*to pay attention*	landen*†	*to land*
aufräumen *sep*	*to tidy up*	legen	*to put (down)*
aufwachen *sep*	*to wake up*	lernen	*to learn*
ausmachen *sep*	*to switch off*	machen	*to make, do*
auspacken *sep*	*to unpack*	meinen	*to think, say*
sich beeilen†	*to hurry*	melden†	*to announce, register*
begrüßen†	*to greet*	mieten†	*to rent*
besichtigen†	*to visit*	nähen	*to sew*
bestellen†	*to order*	öffnen†	*to open*
besuchen†	*to visit*	organisieren†	*to organise*
bezahlen†	*to pay*	parken	*to park*
brauchen	*to need*	planen	*to plan*
buchen	*to book*	prüfen	*to test, check*
danken + Dat	*to thank*	rauchen	*to smoke*
decken	*to cover, set (table)*	regnen†	*to rain*
drücken	*to press, push*	reisen*	*to travel*
einkaufen *sep*	*to shop*	reparieren†	*to repair*
einpacken *sep*	*to pack*	sagen	*to say*
erlauben†	*to allow*	sammeln	*to collect*
fehlen	*to be missing*	schauen	*to look*
fragen	*to ask*	schicken	*to send*
sich freuen	*to be pleased*	schmecken	*to taste*
gestatten†	*to permit*	schneien	*to snow*
glauben	*to think, believe*	segeln	*to sail*
gucken	*to look*	sparen	*to save*
heiraten†	*to marry*	starten†	*to start*
sich hinsetzen *sep*	*to sit down*	stecken	*to put (in)*
hoffen	*to hope*		

* takes *sein* in the Perfect tense   *sep* indicates separable verb
† verb with slight irregularity (see pages 50, 52)   *insep* indicates inseparable verb

German Grammar — Verbs

Regular Verbs (continued)

Infinitive	Meaning	Infinitive	Meaning
stellen	*to put (upright)*	versuchen†	*to try, attempt*
eine Frage stellen	*to ask a question*	vorbereiten† *sep*	*to prepare*
stimmen	*to be right*	sich vorstellen *sep*	*to introduce oneself*
suchen	*to look for*	wählen	*to choose*
tanken	*to fill up with petrol*	warten†	*to wait*
teilen	*to share*	wechseln	*to change (money)*
telefonieren†	*to phone*	wiederholen *insep*	*to repeat*
träumen	*to dream*	wohnen	*to live*
turnen	*to do gymnastics*	wünschen	*to wish*
üben	*to practise*	zahlen	*to pay*
überraschen *insep*	*to surprise*	zeichnen†	*to draw*
verdienen†	*to earn*	zeigen	*to show*
verkaufen†	*to sell*	zuhören *sep*	*to listen to*
vermieten†	*to rent out*		

* takes *sein* in the Perfect tense
† verb with slight irregularity (see pages 50, 52)
sep indicates separable verb
insep indicates inseparable verb

Examples of Tenses of Regular Verbs

Infinitive	Present	Imperfect	Perfect	Meaning
spielen	ich spiele	ich spielte	ich habe gespielt	*to play*
besuchen†	ich besuche	ich besuchte	ich habe besucht	*to visit*
warten†	er wartet	ich wartete	ich habe gewartet	*to wait*
abholen *sep*	ich hole ... ab	ich holte ... ab	ich habe abgeholt	*to fetch*
wiederholen *insep*	ich wiederhole	ich wiederholte	ich habe wiederholt	*to repeat*

Irregular Verb Table — German Grammar

Verbs with separable or inseparable prefixes and with the prefixes be-, emp-, ent-, er-, ge-, miss-, ver- and zer- should be looked up without their prefix. * denotes verb with *sein* in perfect and other compound tenses.

Infinitive	3rd Person Present	Imperfect	Perfect	Meaning
backen	**bäckt**	backte	gebacken	*to bake*
befehlen	**befiehlt**	befahl	befohlen	*to command*
begießen	begießt	begoss	begossen	*to water (plants)*
beginnen	beginnt	begann	begonnen	*to begin*
beißen	beißt	biss	gebissen	*to bite*
bersten	**birst**	barst	geborsten*	*to burst*
beschließen	beschließt	beschloss	beschlossen	*to decide*
beschreiben	beschreibt	beschrieb	beschrieben	*to describe*
biegen	biegt	bog	gebogen	*to bend*
bieten	**bietet**	bot	geboten	*to offer*
binden	**bindet**	band	gebunden	*to fasten*
bitten (um)	**bittet (um)**	bat (um)	(um) gebeten	*to ask (for)*
blasen	**bläst**	blies	geblasen	*to blow*
bleiben	bleibt	blieb	geblieben*	*to stay*
braten	**brät**	briet	gebraten	*to roast*
brechen	**bricht**	brach	gebrochen	*to break*
brennen	brennt	brannte	gebrannt	*to burn*
bringen	bringt	brachte	gebracht	*to bring*
denken	denkt	dachte	gedacht	*to think*

German Grammar — Irregular Verb Table

Infinitive	3rd Person Present	Imperfect	Perfect	Meaning
dürfen	**darf**	durfte		*to be allowed to*
empfehlen	**empfiehlt**	empfahl	empfohlen	*to recommend*
erschrecken	**erschrickt**	erschrak	erschrocken	*to terrify*
essen	**isst**	aß	gegessen	*to eat*
fahren	**fährt**	fuhr	gefahren*	*to travel*
fallen	**fällt**	fiel	gefallen*	*to fall*
fangen	**fängt**	fing	gefangen	*to catch*
finden	**findet**	fand	gefunden	*to find*
fliegen	fliegt	flog	geflogen*	*to fly*
frieren	friert	fror	gefroren	*to freeze*
geben	**gibt**	gab	gegeben	*to give*
gehen	geht	ging	gegangen*	*to go*
gelingen	gelingt	gelang	gelungen*	*to succeed*
genießen	genießt	genoss	genossen	*to enjoy*
geschehen	**geschieht**	geschah	geschehen*	*to happen*
gewinnen	gewinnt	gewann	gewonnen	*to win*
greifen	greift	griff	gegriffen	*to grasp*
haben	**hat**	hatte	gehabt	*to have*
halten	**hält**	hielt	gehalten	*to stop, to hold*
hängen	hängt	hing	gehangen	*to hang*
heben	hebt	hob	gehoben	*to lift*
heißen	heißt	hieß	geheißen	*to be called*

Irregular Verb Table — German Grammar

Infinitive	3rd Person Present	Imperfect	Perfect	Meaning
helfen	**hilft**	half	geholfen	to help
kennen	kennt	kannte	gekannt	to know
kommen	kommt	kam	gekommen*	to come
können	**kann**	konnte		to be able to
laden	**lädt**	lud	geladen	load
lassen	**lässt**	ließ	gelassen	to leave
laufen	**läuft**	lief	gelaufen*	to run
leiden	**leidet**	litt	gelitten	suffer
leihen	leiht	lieh	geliehen	to lend
lesen	**liest**	las	gelesen	to read
liegen	liegt	lag	gelegen	to lie
liegen lassen	lässt liegen	ließ liegen	liegen lassen	to leave lying around
messen	**misst**	maß	gemessen	to measure
mögen	**mag**	mochte		to like to
müssen	**muss**	musste		to have to
nehmen	**nimmt**	nahm	genommen	to take
nennen	nennt	nannte	genannt	to name
pfeifen	pfeift	pfiff	gepfiffen	whistle
raten	**rät**	riet	geraten	to guess
reiben	reibt	rieb	gerieben	to rub
reißen	reißt	riss	gerissen	to tear
reiten	**reitet**	ritt	geritten*	to ride

German Grammar — Irregular Verb Table

Infinitive	3rd Person Present	Imperfect	Perfect	Meaning
riechen	riecht	roch	gerochen	*to smell*
rufen	ruft	rief	gerufen	*to call*
scheiden	**scheidet**	schied	geschieden	*to part*
scheinen	scheint	schien	geschienen	*to shine, to seem*
schießen	schießt	schoß	geschossen	*to shoot*
schieben	schiebt	schob	geschoben	*to push*
schlafen	**schläft**	schlief	geschlafen	*to sleep*
schlagen	**schlägt**	schlug	geschlagen	*to hit*
schleichen	schleicht	schlich	geschlichen*	*to creep*
schließen	schließt	schloss	geschlossen	*to shut*
schneiden	**schneidet**	schnitt	geschnitten	*to cut*
schreiben	schreibt	schrieb	geschrieben	*to write*
schreien	schreit	schrie	geschrieen	*to shout*
schweigen	schweigt	schwieg	geschwiegen	*to be silent*
schwimmen	schwimmt	schwamm	geschwommen(*)	*to swim*
sehen	**sieht**	sah	gesehen	*to see*
sein	**ist**	war	gewesen*	*to be*
singen	singt	sang	gesungen	*to sing*
sinken	sinkt	sank	gesunken*	*to sink*
sitzen	sitzt	saß	gesessen	*to sit*
sollen	**soll**	sollte		*to be supposed to, to ought to*

Irregular Verb Table

Infinitive	3rd Person Present	Imperfect	Perfect	Meaning
sprechen	**spricht**	sprach	gesprochen	to speak
springen	springt	sprang	gesprungen*	to jump
stechen	**sticht**	stoch	gestochen	sting
stehen	steht	stand	gestanden	to stand
stehlen	**stiehlt**	stahl	gestohlen	to steal
sterben	**stirbt**	starb	gestorben*	to die
steigen	steigt	stieg	gestiegen*	to climb
stinken	stinkt	stank	gestunken	to smell
stoßen	**stößt**	stieß	gestoßen*	to bump
streichen	streicht	strich	gestrichen	to cancel
sich streiten	streitet	stritt	gestritten	to argue
tragen	**trägt**	trug	getragen	to carry, wear
treffen	**trifft**	traf	getroffen	to meet, to hit
treiben	treibt	trieb	getrieben	to do (sport)
treten	**tritt**	trat	getreten*	to step
trinken	trinkt	trank	getrunken	to drink
tun	**tut**	tat	getan	to do
verbringen	verbringt	verbrachte	verbracht	to spend time
vergessen	**vergisst**	vergaß	vergessen	to forget
vergleichen	vergleicht	verglich	verglichen	to compare
verlassen	**verlässt**	verließ	verlassen	to leave
verlieren	verliert	verlor	verloren	to lose

German Grammar — Irregular Verb Table

Infinitive	3rd Person Present	Imperfect	Perfect	Meaning
vermeiden	**vermeidet**	vermied	vermieden	to avoid
verschleißen	verschleißt	verschliss	verschlissen	to wear out
verschwinden	**verschwindet**	verschwand	verschwunden*	to disappear
wachsen	**wächst**	wuchs	gewachsen*	to grow
waschen	**wäscht**	wusch	gewaschen	to wash
weisen	weist	wies	gewiesen	to show
werben	wirbt	warb	geworben	to attract
werden	**wird**	wurde	geworden*	to become
werfen	**wirft**	warf	geworfen	to throw
wiegen	wiegt	wog	gewogen	weigh
wissen	**weiß**	wusste	gewusst	to know
wollen	**will**	wollte		to want to
ziehen	zieht	zog	gezogen	to pull
zwingen	zwingt	zwang	gezwungen	to force

Index

1 - 2 - 3 rule 45
aber 20
abstract nouns 2
accusative 1, 15
accusative reflexive pronouns 38
active verbs 5
active voice 57
adjective endings: tables 1, 2, 3 6-7
adjectives 1, 6-9
adjectives used as nouns 8, 74
adverbs 1, 10-11
adverbs ending in -*s* 24
agent in the passive 60
agreement 1
alle 6
alles 41
als 19, 21
anstatt ... zu 71
articles 1, 12-14
Ausrufezeichen 44
auxiliary verb 5
Bedingungssätze 62
bleiben 15
capital letters 43
cardinal numbers 31
cases and their use 15-17, 40
clause 2
clock times 23
co-ordinating conjunction 44-45
comma 20, 43
command forms 64
commands 5, 44
common nouns 2
comparative 1
comparative phrases 72
comparisons 18-19
compound nouns - gender 28
concrete nouns 2
conditions 62
conjugation 4
conjunctions 2, 20-21
da 10
dass 39
dates 22
dates and times 22-24
dative 1, 17
dative and accusative word order 47
dative reflexive pronouns 38

days 22
declension of nouns 29
definite and indefinite time 15, 24
definite article 1,12
dein 7
demonstrative pronouns 3, 42
denn 20
derjenige, etc 42
dieser 6, 12, 42
direct object 15
direct object pronouns 3
direct speech 44
dort 10
du or *Sie*? 38
du-commands 64
durch 60
dürfen 67
ein paar 7
einige 7
er, sie, es 39
etwas 9, 41
euer 7
exclamations 44, 72
first person 48
fractions 33
Fragewörter 11
future tense 4, 51
gender 2
gender of nouns 25
general before specific - word order .. 47
genitive 1, 16
greetings 16
Großbuchstaben 43
haben or *sein*? 54
heißen 15
-*her* 10
Herz 30
hier 10
Hilfsverb 5
-*hin* 10
ihr 7
ihr-commands 64
imperatives 5, 64
imperfect tense 4, 54-55
impersonal expressions 17
impersonal verbs 75
indefinite article 1, 13-14
indefinite pronouns 3

German Grammar — Index

indefinite time 24
indefinite time expressions 16
indirect object 17
indirect object pronouns 3
infinitive 3, 48, 70
infinitive used as noun 73
infinitive with *zu* 70
infinitive without *zu* 72
inseparable verbs 79
interrogative pronouns 3, 41
irgend- 10
irregular verbs 4, 48
jeder 6, 12, 42
jener 6, 12, 42
Julei 22
Juno 22
kein 7
Konjuntiv 63
Konjuntiv II 62
können 67
Let's 64
letter openings 44
lists 43
loan words from English 28
main clause 2
man 61
mancher 6, 12, 42
mehrere 7
mein 7
mit 60
mixed verbs 4, 49
modal verbs 46, 63, 65-69
mögen 68
months 22
müssen 68
nichts 9, 41
nominative 1, 15
nothing and something 9
nouns 2, 25-30
nouns - plural forms 28
nouns -gender 25-28
number 2
numbers 7, 31-33
oben 10
object 4
oder 20
ohne ... zu 70
open conditions 62
ordinal numbers 32
participles 73

Partizip Perfekt 73
passive - alternatives 61
passive infinitive 70
passive verbs 5
passive voice 57
past participle 5, 73
perfect tense 4, 52
personal pronouns 3, 37
persons 48
pluperfect tense 4, 56
plural 2
plural of nouns 28
Plusquamperfekt 4, 56
possessions 16
possessive adjectives 7
possibilities 62
Präteritum 4, 54
prepositions 2, 34-36
present participle 5, 74
present tense 4, 49
pronoun before noun - word order ... 47
pronouns 3, 37-42
proper nouns 2
punctuation 43
question words 11
questions 46
reflexive pronouns 38
reflexive verbs 5, 76
reflexives instead of passive 61
regular verb list 82
regular verbs 4, 48
relative pronoun agreement 40
relative pronouns 3, 39
requests 63
Saxon genitive 16
scheinen 15
second person 48
sein 7, 15, 50, 54, 65
sein-passive 59
separable or unseparable verbs 79
separable prefixes 78
separable verb 46, 78
sie 39
Sie or *du*? 38
Sie-commands 64
simple past tense 54
singular 2
small ads 72
solcher 6, 12
sollen 69

Index

sondern 20
Sonnabend 22
special days and seasons 23
spelling and punctuation 43-44
spelling changes in nouns 29
ss 43
ß 43
statt ... zu 71
strong verbs 4, 48
subject 4, 15
subject pronouns 3
subjunctive 63
subordinate clause 2, 44
subordinating conjunction 45, 20
superlative 1, 18
telling the time 23
tenses 4
that 39
third person 48
time, manner, place 46
trennbare Verben 78
um ... zu 70
Umlaut 43
und 20
unhelpful genders of human beings ... 28
unser 7
unten 10
verb - comma - verb 44
verbs 3, 48-88

verbs followed by a preposition 80
verbs followed by dative 75
verbs followed by nominative 74
viele 7
von 60
wann 21
weak nouns 29
weak verb list 82
weak verbs 4, 48
weak, strong and mixed verbs 48
weiß, ich weiß 50
welcher 6, 12, 41
wenn 21
werden 15, 51
werden-passive 57
when 21
which 39
who? 41
whose 40
wie 19
wishes 63
wissen 50
wollen 69
word order 45, 45-47, 66
words following the *der die das* pattern
 12
words following the *ein eine ein* pattern
 14
year 23